LOVE ADDICTION WORKBOOK

LOVE
ADDICTION
Workbook

EVIDENCE-BASED TOOLS TO SUPPORT
RECOVERY AND HELP YOU BUILD
HEALTHY LONG-TERM RELATIONSHIPS

DR. HOWARD C. SAMUELS

R
ROCKRIDGE
PRESS

For general information on our other products and services or to obtain technical support, please contact our Customer Care Department within the United States at (866) 744-2665, or outside the United States at (510) 253-0500.

Rockridge Press publishes its books in a variety of electronic and print formats. Some content that appears in print may not be available in electronic books, and vice versa.

TRADEMARKS: Rockridge Press and the Rockridge Press logo are trademarks or registered trademarks of Callisto Media Inc. and/or its affiliates, in the United States and other countries, and may not be used without written permission. All other trademarks are the property of their respective owners. Rockridge Press is not associated with any product or vendor mentioned in this book.

Interior and Cover Designer: Amanda Kirk
Art Producer: Janice Ackerman
Editor: Jed Bickman
Production Editor: Andrew Yackira
Production Manager: Riley Hoffman

Illustration: Copyright © Kamila Hyhlikova /shutterstock
Author photo courtesy of Duke Shoman

ISBN: Print 978-1-64876-855-2
eBook 978-1-64876-856-9
R0

This book is dedicated to anyone for whom
love has proved an illusion, and to my children,
Cooper, Greer, and Chase Samuels, whose
existence is, to me, not only proof that
love is real but—more importantly—
that I am capable of it
if I do the work.

Contents

INTRODUCTION viii

CHAPTER ONE

Understanding Love Addiction

xii

CHAPTER TWO

Start Your Road to Recovery

24

CHAPTER THREE

Identify Your Beliefs

42

CHAPTER FOUR

Connect with Your Feelings

68

CHAPTER FIVE

Change Your Relationships

98

CHAPTER SIX

Practice Self-Care

128

CHAPTER SEVEN

Keep Up the Momentum

155

Resources 169

References 170

Index 171

INTRODUCTION

———

I MET A GIRL AND SHE CHANGED MY LIFE. Looking back on it, I can
remember everything about her with an intensity that feels as if we'd only
just met yesterday. I remember the way sunlight bounced off her hair; the
flash of her throat when she laughed; how it felt to hold her, kiss her; the
inimitable way her body felt when we lay together; the weight of her head
on my chest when we slept; the way she looked at me when I spoke, the way
I hung on to every word she said . . .

And then one day, seemingly out of nowhere, she told me that our relationship had run its course for her and that it was over.

Her reasons were sound. She said remaining together would not be fair to
either one of us, and then she simply kissed me on the cheek, told me what a
remarkable man I was, and walked away.

And that was when I fell apart.

I was in such a dark place, it frightened not only myself but my closest
friends. We would go out to restaurants or nightclubs and I would fall apart,
sobbing over this relationship that had defined who I was as a man, as a
person. On any given night, my friends would draw straws in the parking lot
to see who would walk Howard to his car and console him.

It was humiliating, yes, but I believed in my feelings. She was the love
of my life, and she didn't love me back, which in turn informed my belief
that I was unlovable and would forever be alone. This went on for about a
month, with me isolating in my apartment, eating my feelings (overeating or

not eating enough, depending on the day), and calling friends at all hours as I pored over every detail of our relationship, trying senselessly to figure out what I'd done wrong, what I'd said wrong.

But I need to tell you one vital detail: *She and I had been dating for only three months.* Three months, and I was experiencing what I can refer to only as Insanity Pain. Not even the death of my own father had affected me this greatly!

Soon thereafter, I saw her with her friends at a coffee shop we frequented (Los Angeles, despite its breadth, is actually little more than a big small town, as anyone who lives there can attest), and I immediately shifted the conversation at my table to talking about *her* and *her* problems with commitment and intimacy, all within earshot of her table. Eventually, she simply got up and left, flashing me a look that asked, "*Are you crazy?*" Which begged the question: Was I?

The answer was yes. My feelings weren't imaginary; they were real. But once I shone the light inward, I realized (with a lot of help) that *she* wasn't the one with intimacy issues—*I* was. I looked at my life and the wreckage of my past relationships and realized *she* didn't have commitment issues; *I* did.

What a game changer that realization was! It wasn't as if I'd had some magic tome to refer to at the time, either. These were the '80s, and the world wasn't ripe with information like it is now. I had no Dr. Phil, no Oprah to walk me through my pain or help me identify my feelings. All I had were my friends and classmates, who meant well but were also still just learning about the Human Experience for themselves. There was no such thing as a Love Addiction Workbook, and so, as I ventured back out into the world and continued to be dashed against the rocks by failed relationship after failed relationship, I made a mental note that yes, there should be one: a book for people like us. And that's what this is.

At the heart of every addiction sits unbridled anguish coupled with a sense of futility—an inner voice that says, "Well, here's another fine mess you've gotten us into." In fact, that's what happens: You wake up emotionally disorganized and in very real anguish, and you realize that once again you have placed yourself in a position to be hurt. And you are clueless as to why or how it happened, but here you are again.

Many think of hell as torture and fire and brimstone. But novelist Stephen King made popular the definition of what I believe to be the cornerstone of addiction. According to him, hell might just be repetition. And once you're able to see the forest for the trees, the first thing you want to do is step out of the woods and into the sunlight of the spirit. You want to break the cycle.

This is a book to help you do just that. I am a dedicated psychotherapist whose motive remains helping people. I am also a man who, in his heart, does not want to see anyone suffer. Especially not when I myself know what that suffering feels like. And not when I myself know the anodyne.

Each of us is a constellation of experiences and, sometimes, traumas that comprise who and why we are, but we need not be imprisoned by them. We can learn and grow from them and—if we're willing to do the work—free ourselves from the anguish of repeated behaviors and *find ways to rise above our stars*.

Socrates believed that the better we know ourselves, the easier it is to know what we want, reason with our inner selves, and, in doing so, find happiness. Working together through this book, you and I are going to employ a Socratic method of poring over concepts and ideas that will help cast a blinding light on the things that cause us to repeatedly fall into the same traps. And by enlisting a variety of proven techniques like cognitive behavioral therapy (CBT), mindfulness, and motivational interviewing, we will realize that we aren't abandoned, broken toys—we are powerful people who desperately want to change and grow and heal, and we are entirely capable of same.

Granted, this workbook will never replace therapy, but the strategies and techniques in this book can be a terrific starting point or even be used in addition to therapy and support group sessions.

As Johann Hari, author of *Chasing the Scream*, so eloquently stated, "The opposite of addiction isn't sobriety, it is human connection." I am here to tell you, connection is not something we mindlessly crave. Connection is what we deserve. And we can all have healthy, rewarding, enduring relationships.

Let's do this!

CHAPTER ONE

Understanding Love Addiction

Have you ever wondered why we choose the people that we do, over and over again? Or why we never seem to be truly happy in relationships? Some of us choose partners who are incredibly narcissistic and who would be hard-pressed to even consider that we, too, have needs. Others choose not to have partners at all but rather avoid connection by investing their time and energy in pursuing those who are physically or emotionally unavailable. It's a confusing notion to accept—that maybe we aren't in control of choosing our partners at all or that, perhaps, there are psychological forces at work that compel us to do the things we do time and time again. Before we delve wholly into the work, we need to understand what we are up against and be able to truly understand the enemy within.

WHAT IS LOVE ADDICTION?

In every therapist's academic career, the question of addiction always surfaces amid a veil of conflicting ideas and theorems. The bottom line is that addiction is usually best defined as repeated behaviors that are performed despite any and all negative consequences.

That said, I'd like to welcome you to your love life.

Unlike other addictive or compulsive behavior patterns such as alcoholism or gambling, where consequences are as blatant as a DUI or bankruptcy, love addiction is not as easily self-diagnosed. If that were the case, there would not be as many people suffering from it—people who find themselves lost in patterns laid down during their youth that have become the maze they are forced to walk in adulthood.

Love addiction usually manifests as an addiction to an unavailable person. Many love addicts grew up with parents who were emotionally unavailable to them. This can happen in any family, but it's common in alcoholic families. A child who grows up with emotionally unavailable parents will associate that feeling with love. As they grow up, they then get attracted to individuals who inspire the same feelings that the person experienced in their childhood. Unconsciously, they are drawn to individuals who are aloof, who aren't in touch with their feelings, who are abusive, or who they chase emotionally, resulting in extremely unhealthy relationships caused by always chasing emotionally unavailable people, just as they'd become accustomed to as a child.

On the other hand, when an emotionally available person comes into their life, the love addict tends to pull away, saying things like, "They're boring," "There's no spark," or "There's no attraction." But the reality is that they're experiencing a totally unfamiliar connection—it doesn't affect them as profoundly, nor in the same way, as an emotionally unavailable person.

This is one example of how emotional triggers work. Our mind establishes connections between our past and present experiences, and these connections inform our decision-making in relationships. Love addiction is a kaleidoscope of sophisticated desires hardwired into one driving need: to do the same thing over and over again while expecting different results. So let's try something *new*.

Most love addicts are totally unaware of their patterns and why they exist. They need to learn how to start bringing in emotionally available people, which, in the beginning, is very hard, so they have to work on their intimacy issues because this is a very common intimacy problem for many, many people. And it affects men as much as it does women.

Behavioral addiction and substance addiction are alike in that the cornerstone of both is a sophisticated immediate-reward system they employ in conjunction with a lack of impulse control. For example, once the heroin addict wants that heroin, they will do whatever it takes to get it. It doesn't matter how dire the circumstance—a heroin addict will sacrifice everything to get the heroin. With behavioral addiction, things are a bit more nuanced because the reward is different; the love addict is driven by the need for an emotional "fix." As in the case with the girl who broke my heart, it was never about her; it was always about me and my behavior. This is why a lot of the therapy around love addiction rarely addresses the object of our desire; the therapy usually addresses *us*.

The treatment for love addiction begins by taking a long, hard look at yourself and the fact that you are set in your ways after accumulating years of negative behavior. And because you have such an ingrained pattern of negative behavior, it is extremely difficult to shatter that pattern.

Most love addicts have engaged in *years* of this reinforced behavior, and many are resistant to breaking the pattern. They will justify this by saying things like, "But I love him/her," having no clue that it is not love at all but an addiction born from the real or perceived abuse and neglect they encountered as children.

Issues in adult relationships can often be traced back to childhood experiences. For many of us, the following childhood experiences may have contributed to our becoming love addicts:

→ Separation or divorce of parents

→ Alcoholism in the household, involving one or both parents

→ Child abuse

→ Neglect

→ Repeated abandonment

→ Losing a sibling or parent at a young age

→ Being adopted

→ Having parents who were immature, shut down, or emotionally unavailable

→ Lack of positive validation or support from parents

Together, with the help of this workbook, you and I will first take a look at your own relationships to determine whether or not you are a love addict. Next, after performing an autopsy on your love life (past and present), we'll try to get to the root of why you are continually placing yourself in a position to be hurt.

Love addiction is an Equal Opportunity Destroyer. It ruins every life it touches and thrives on the insanity and despair it induces. But you are not alone. There is hope for us, and at the end of the day, we all deserve to be happy and adored.

LOVE VS. SEX ADDICTION

Both love addiction and sex addiction are intimacy disorders, usually developed to cope with trauma, abuse, or neglect that one experienced while still very young. Sex and love addiction create the distance needed in order for one to feel safe.

The sex addict will use sex as a replacement for intimacy, creating a barrier between themselves and their respective partners by limiting the interaction to just that: sex. The love addict will choose unavailable partners as well, presumably to waylay the threat of rejection or abandonment. If you invest feelings in someone who is unavailable, emotionally or otherwise, you take rejection off the table. The love addict cannot live in the truth yet; they find themselves in emotionally charged relationships where there are mixed signals or pining away for people who are unavailable. Why climb into the ring and risk a bloody nose when you can watch from the cheap seats and romanticize about what it would be like to have that person's affections for real?

Marriage family therapist Alexandra Katehakis, PhD gives the following succinct descriptors in her *Psychology Today* article, "Sex and Love Addiction: What's the Difference?"

The criteria of sex addiction include:

- Preoccupation with sexual behavior or preparatory activities
- Inordinate amount of time spent obtaining sex, being sexual, or recovering from sexual experiences
- Needing to increase the intensity, frequency, number, or risk level of behaviors to achieve the desired effect
- Distress, anxiety, restlessness, or irritability if unable to engage in the behavior

A partial list of love addiction symptoms includes:

- Inability to stop seeing a specific person despite knowing that the person is destructive to you
- Getting "high" from romance, fantasy, or intrigue
- Having relationships to try to deal with or escape from life's problems
- Feeling desperation or uneasiness when away from a lover or sexual partner

Deep Dive

SELF QUIZ: AM I A LOVE ADDICT?

Throughout this workbook, you'll have opportunities to dig deep and investigate different aspects of love addiction. These "Deep Dives" should not be approached with a cavalier attitude. I encourage you to pause and really consider your responses before committing them to pen and paper.

With this quiz, think a moment and reflect on your answer before checking the corresponding box. Tell the truth. Honesty is the only weapon you have right now, and it's a sword that will cut through the veil of lies that keep you in anguish, and that's okay. It's okay to feel pain. It's okay to feel shame. I'm right here with you, and I promise I am not judging you. I know and understand that for some of you, this quiz will be a cakewalk. But for many of you, completing it will be nothing short of heroic.

1. I usually develop crushes on unavailable people.

    ☐ TRUE
    ☐ FALSE

2. I find myself trapped in "on-again/off-again" relationships where I need them more than they need me.

    ☐ TRUE
    ☐ FALSE

3. I often fantasize about having sex with people who are unavailable or have no idea how I secretly feel about them.

    ☐ TRUE
    ☐ FALSE

4. I experience rejection more often than others because I "put myself out there" with people I know are not attracted to me, are involved with other people, or are simply unavailable.

    ☐ TRUE
    ☐ FALSE

5. I place the needs of my partner ahead of my own.

☐ TRUE
☐ FALSE

6. I often find myself in damaging or abusive relationships.

☐ TRUE
☐ FALSE

7. I often find myself in relationships where I feel sorry for myself and choose to stay anyway despite my unhappiness because they are "worth it."

☐ TRUE
☐ FALSE

8. I am often jealous in a relationship and fear losing my partner to someone else, even though I've got no information to support the potential for infidelity, so I become needy or clingy.

☐ TRUE
☐ FALSE

9. I tend to lose myself in the other person, changing to please or attract them. I cast aside my own beliefs and desires to please them in the hopes of attracting or keeping them.

☐ TRUE
☐ FALSE

10. I tend to become obsessed with people I like, often changing my life in the hopes of being noticed by them at one of their usual haunts or activities. I stalk them on social media. I surreptitiously ask their friends for information about them.

☐ TRUE
☐ FALSE

11. I need "them" to like me because honestly, I don't like myself a lot of the time.

　　☐ TRUE
　　☐ FALSE

12. I will risk humiliation, my job, and my friends just to be with "them."

　　☐ TRUE
　　☐ FALSE

13. I often let my loneliness decide who my partner will be, no matter what my standards are.

　　☐ TRUE
　　☐ FALSE

14. My partner is verbally or physically abusive to me, but I choose to remain in the relationship.

　　☐ TRUE
　　☐ FALSE

15. When a relationship ends, I find myself lost, alone, and despondent. I feel as if no one will ever love me because I am unlovable (a.k.a., *I was lucky to have them and now they are gone*).

　　☐ TRUE
　　☐ FALSE

16. If I'm in a relationship and it becomes comfortable, I will often direct my affections to strangers in the hope of igniting a spark so that I feel validated and adored. I will risk the relationship (or marriage) by flirting with or even having sex with other people so that I can feel the rush of new love.

　　☐ TRUE
　　☐ FALSE

17. Nothing excites me more than winning someone over. I guess I'm in it for the conquest, because once I get what I want, I become bored and feel the need to move on.

    ☐ TRUE
    ☐ FALSE

18. I am extremely needy and emotional and often find myself in relationships with narcissists. It is safer to be little more than an object to them than for them to truly see me and help me work through my issues and become a more complete, empowered person. I hide in unrequited relationships.

    ☐ TRUE
    ☐ FALSE

19. In looking back over my life, many of my long-term relationships have involved my tricking the other person into loving me, usually by fact gathering and becoming the thing I knew they desired. I have done this so often that I have lost myself and feel like a patchwork quilt of everyone I pretended to be in order to feel loved.

    ☐ TRUE
    ☐ FALSE

If you answered TRUE to 10 or more of these questions, chances are you are a love addict.

THE FIVE STEPS OF LOVE ADDICTION

Love addiction has a pattern—a cycle—that can eventually become the maze that entraps us for most of our adult lives. But that cycle is only as powerful as the ignorance that accompanies it. The cycle usually goes like this:

1. **The inciting incident.** Something about someone triggers the attraction. It does not matter whether that attraction is reciprocated; we act on it and fan the flames of our growing addiction to this person, which leads to . . .

2. **Craving the dopamine/oxytocin hit.** Sometimes it occurs when we see the person, but we can also condition ourselves to get the same fix by visiting their social media accounts or frequenting their place of business. A kind word or welcoming smile will often propel us to new heights of euphoria. This, of course, leads us to . . .

3. **Setting up repeated doses.** Things begin to intensify as we take more risks to be near the object of our affection. We change our schedule, develop new hobbies, and even change who we really are just to be near the person. It is titillating to be on the verge of a passionate love affair, and we tend to daydream more and more about what will be the be-all and end-all of any relationship we've ever had. This honeymoon phase is when we are at our happiest because it is also when we are most committed to the fantasy and least likely to allow the reality of the situation to burst our bubble. But it leads to . . .

4. **Painting all the red flags green.** This is usually the worst stage of our addiction, as this is typically when we realize our feelings are not reciprocated. This doesn't deter us, however, as we continue to stoke the flames of our unmet desires by sinking deeper into fantasy while conjuring justifications for the rejection. We move into denial at this stage because we so desperately want the relationship to work. This phase inevitably leads to . . .

5. **The end.** Ground zero. The ultimate death of the dream. Reality is unavoidable. This is the part where the object of our affection rejects us or, horrifically, ends all contact, leaving us confused, devastated, lost, and alone with our grief. This is not the same as a conventional breakup; it is the death of a seed that was never allowed to grow,

leaving us with a despair that grips and immobilizes us, enshrouding us with an anguish that seems to dwarf all others.

It is important to note that most of this occurs via an intimate internal dialogue, and many people around us are not privy to this descent into madness. So, what we wind up with is our own private hell, one we are typically too embarrassed to shed light upon—that is, until we *do the work and invite the help.*

Dopamine and Oxytocin

I believe that two major neurotransmitters—chemicals that your body makes—contribute to the phenomenon of love addiction: dopamine and oxytocin. Dopamine is, among other things, a fundamental component of how we experience pleasure. For our purposes, dopamine is the hormone that makes us feel amazing when we see the object of our affection: We see them and suddenly our system is flooded with it. When we have love addiction, we want that dopamine hit to go on and on and on.

The neurotransmitter oxytocin is nicknamed the "hug drug." A hormone vital in reproduction, oxytocin triggers labor and the release of breast milk in females and the movement of sperm in males. In a 2012 study, it was discovered that couples in the first stages of romantic attachment had significantly higher levels of oxytocin than their single counterparts, tying oxytocin to new love and even the intensity of orgasms.

It is easy to see how we can form such strong attachments to the people we love and, strangely, even stronger attachments to the people we fantasize about. Love, real or imagined, carries with it a powerful punch! Everybody wants that dopamine hit, and oxytocin seems to be the culprit that inspires trust, gazing, empathy, fidelity—we get that "hit," and all logic flies out the window.

SUSAN'S DILEMMA

Susan is in a relationship with a verbally abusive man. She's been living with him for almost two years now. He presents himself as a really nice guy, but he berates her constantly and smashes her dreams—especially dreams that could lead to her financial independence. Still, she loves the attention she gets from her girlfriends and other competing females because he is so rugged and outwardly handsome, and although she spends more time alone at home crying in her bed, she still offers that he is kind to her, lavishing her with flowers and public affection on special occasions as well as romantic getaways and gifts. She says he is her *soul mate*, yet she has never spoken of him apologizing for hurting her feelings or for presenting a negative bias on her dreams and aspirations. And she complains that the sex "isn't all that."

She was a regular at the nightclub she and her friends used to frequent (she no longer goes; he doesn't like seeing her out, but he still goes out alone to "hang out with friends"). Her friends were all enamored by his good looks, but they failed to arouse his attention. Susan began to develop a harmless crush on him and kept tabs on him at the club, rushing to the bar whenever he would go to freshen up his drink, until one night they struck up a conversation. Later, drunk, he drove her home to her apartment and made passionate love to her that ended in minutes when he climaxed.

Within a month, he'd moved in with her. Within six, they'd found an apartment with both of their names on the lease. But it seemed as if, in the entire time she was courting him, she'd developed a fantasy about who he was, and nothing he could do or say would smash that fantasy. In her mind, he was not the abusive, selfish, uninspiring lover she'd become enmeshed with.

In public, they were the perfect couple, but behind closed doors, Susan was a lonely woman who cried herself to sleep every night.

I have been seeing Susan weekly for two months now. The work is not just to get her out of this relationship; it's also to help her look at her life and try to discover why she approached this relationship the way she did, so that the next man she falls in love with will actually be the man she falls in love with rather than a fantasy she's parked her life and her future in. Thankfully, Susan is *ready to do the work*.

Deep Dive

SEEING IS BELIEVING

"When someone shows you who they are,
believe them the first time." **—MAYA ANGELOU**

This is a simple exercise, but it can be harrowing, and it must be done alone. As with many of the Deep Dives, be as honest with yourself as possible. This is a two-week challenge. Continue to read the book, but do this exercise daily. Diligence is key, so hold yourself to it and mark your calendar. Here, you'll look at your behavior in a safe, nonjudgmental space.

1. For two weeks, place a red "X" on the days you and your loved one argue or fight. It doesn't matter what the argument was about, nor who "won." Include the days that you butted heads or that your loved one was the cause of any negative emotions you felt on that day.

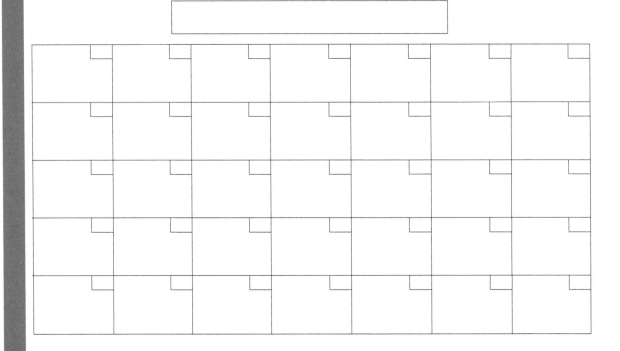

You don't have to be in a relationship to do this exercise. Frame any romantic relationship you've had within the confines of a two-week period and try to remember what it was like. We are performing an autopsy on the relationship so we can get a bird's-eye view of what it is (or was) really like for you to be with this person, so try to be as thorough as possible in this endeavor.

2. If you are single, place a red "X" on the days where you took an action to feel closer to the unavailable object of your affection. Did you scroll through their social media feeds for the hundredth time? Did you manipulate people or events so you could be near this person? Did you contrive a reason to establish contact with this person, just so you could hear their voice, receive a text message back, or hang out with them?

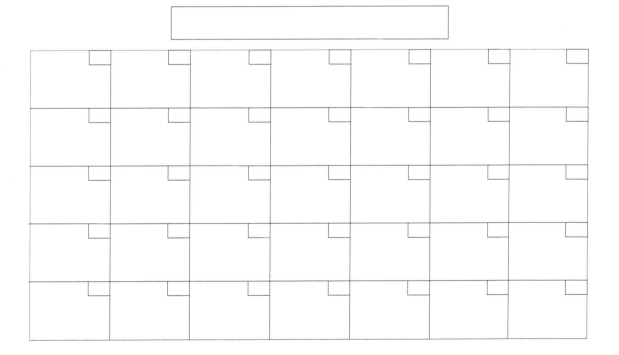

3. Each day of the same two weeks, write the name of someone you were physically or emotionally intimate with in the past. This does not need to have ended with sex; it might simply be someone you dated or loved from afar. Write their name and how you felt about them and, more importantly, how they felt about you. Limit the latter specifically to their words and their actions; stay away from fantasy.

NAME	WHAT WE MEANT TO EACH OTHER

JUST THE FACTS, MA'AM

On page 9, we talked about love addiction as a cycle with five steps. Choose one relationship you've had and see if you can break it down into these five stages. Be as honest as possible in thoroughly detailing the events and circumstances of the failed romantic endeavor. Include any mixed signals you may have received and how you interpreted and acted upon them. If this model doesn't match your story, think about what's different.

1. The inciting incident:

....

....

....

....

....

....

....

....

2. How did I get my "fix"?

....

....

....

....

....

....

....

....

3. What did I change about myself or my life for this person?

....

....

....

....

....

....

....

....

4. What red flags did I ignore about this person as I indulged in the fantasy of our lives together, and why did I ignore them?

....

....

....

....

....

....

....

....

....

5. How did it end? What did it do to me? What was the consequence?

....

....

....

....

....

....

....

....

....

LOVE ON THE BRAIN

Earlier we discussed the biochemical reactions that occur when we fall in love, and it became easy to see how the feelings generated by these chemical reactions inform all of our decision-making. It doesn't make it any easier to *not* make those decisions, does it?

Didn't think so.

Hell is repetition, remember? And the definition of addiction is repeated behavior despite negative consequences. So, how do we recover? Where is the healing? Where is the growth?

Basically, neural pathways are networks of neurons in the brain that communicate with the nervous system and control a host of functions. They are essential to day-to-day living, and when they malfunction, it can result in any number of maladies, including Parkinson's disease and multiple sclerosis. But the main pathway to consider here is the reward pathway. Anytime we encounter an external stimulus that the human experience categorizes as "rewarding," our brain raises the concentration of dopamine in our system.

If the suffering love addict gets a dopamine hit every time they visit, let's say, their crush's Instagram account, then they are going to always associate the mild euphoria with said crush's Instagram account. Left to their own devices, the suffering love addict will relive the fantasy again and again by visiting the same account and viewing the same posts over and over again throughout the course of the day. That's how we condition ourselves to return to the same empty well for water: through repetition.

But there is a solution. A lot of what we do in regards to neural pathways is setting up automatic systems for ourselves. Every morning, when I put my pants on, I do it one leg at a time—*and I always start with my right leg, not my left.*

Think of Little Red Riding Hood. She used to walk to Grandma's house through the woods. She did this so many times that eventually *a path was ground into the forest floor.* Now imagine she decides to use a different route, back and forth, back and forth. Eventually, she will wear a new path into the ground, *and grass will grow over the old path.*

This is the same principle we will explore as we move forward through this workbook. As we learn more about what makes us tick, we will discover new ways to sidestep the things that keep us grounded in anguish and misery and move closer to the things that make us truly happy. And by happy, I mean HAPPY, not merely dopamine addicted, as we have been for so long now.

But it's up to you to take action.

It's up to you to change your life.

Ready? I'll walk with you.

Deep Dive

I THINK, THEREFORE I AM

Start by hacking your thinking. Every day, during a meal, recite the following affirmations. Don't do it in the car; don't do it in the shower; do it while you are replenishing your body. Pick one meal and speak your affirmations while you are eating.

And believe them.

Here they are:

1. Fear of not getting what I want, or losing what I already have, should never motivate my decisions.

2. I am lovable. This is a FACT. I do not need any one person to love me to learn this; in and of myself, I am worthy of love and attention.

3. I have the power to be my authentic self, and that has always been enough, regardless of what I was told or taught. My destiny is not tied to anyone who walked away from me.

4. I am a real person with a real life, and my life will never be as it is on television or in the movies.

5. Only two factors matter at the beginning of any relationship: timing and chemistry. If I don't like someone, it doesn't make them less of a person or unworthy of love. The axiom goes both ways. I afford myself the luxury of picking and choosing who I like; I will let others have the same luxury. It is okay for my feelings to be unrequited; it says nothing about my worth nor my right to be loved. I am allowed to move on unscathed by another.

6. Relationships are hard. That's why many of us are not *in* them. But, just for today, *I will not pursue someone who is unavailable* because I know that doing so means that I am running from true intimacy, which I deserve.

WHAT'S IMPORTANT
FOR YOUR RECOVERY?

ACCEPTANCE. It may sound corny, but acceptance is the cornerstone of every therapeutic exercise I know. Like courage, acceptance is vital to recovery. If you're reading this book, you've already accepted that you have a problem and that you need help. What that looks like is different for every individual, but it all translates into: "Am I willing to look at the part I am playing in my own unhappiness, and am I willing to move into acceptance that perhaps I can have a better love life?"

AN ACCOUNTABILI-BUDDY. In treatment, this would most likely be your therapist. Basically, it is your "person"—the one who holds you accountable so you do what you say you are going to do. It should always be someone you trust with the whole truth. This is extremely difficult because it means you will need to open up to another person in a way that feels safe. "I am going to not check so-and-so's Insta-gram" is an admission of something you might do on a daily basis. Explaining to someone that you are secretly infatuated or in love with this person may be complicated. But couching it in "I need to make my feelings more 'right-sized' so I can seek real relationships with other (available) people" might help. Accountabili-buddies are usu-ally most useful when you're ready to take those first precious steps toward change. Although they are on the horizon for many of us, it is important to screen them and ultimately choose someone you trust and respect.

TRUST IN THE PROCESS. Education is our most important weapon, insofar as the knowledge of what the cycle is helps us rise above it and free ourselves from behaviors that keep us mired in misery. Understanding what is happening to us enables us to be vigilant for the setbacks that attempt to ruin our recovery.

HOW THIS BOOK WILL HELP

There's an old joke that asks, "How many therapists does it take to change a light bulb?" The answer is "One. But the light bulb has to *want* to change."

This book is as innocuous as any other. It's just a few exercises and a lot of information, all wrapped up in a neat little package for you to read and understand. But finding success through this book is all about action. You can't think your way out of addiction; believe me, I know this for a fact.

For success, it's necessary to commit contrary action. This means taking action that is contrary to what you would normally do.

Looking at some of the exercises or perusing them in your head may make them seem trite or ineffectual at first, but that's only because you haven't given a name to your addiction.

Your addiction is your Beast. And the Beast will tell you—always—"Don't do the work. Look at it; it's stupid. How is this supposed to help you not be in pain anymore?"

The Beast wants the power. The Beast wants you alone and feeling sorry for yourself. The Beast wants you to spend your life chasing after unavailable people or trapped in relationships where the only payoffs for your devotions are pain and anguish.

The Beast wants you to listen to all of the horrible inner voices you've been listening to your whole life—voices that tell you that you're useless or unworthy of true love.

Voices that tell you you're ugly.

"No one will ever love you because you're in a wheelchair."

"No one will ever love you because you're just a man in a dress."

"No one will ever love you because you're fat."

"No one will ever love you because you're poor."

"No one will ever love you because you're different."

"No one will ever love you. Who are you kidding? Put. The book. Down."

But I'm encouraging you to hold on to this book and try something different.

Because this book is like Ex-Lax.

You don't need to believe that Ex-Lax will work. You can focus all of your time and energy on believing that it's just a piece of chocolate.

But I can promise you, if you take Ex-Lax, *it will work*.

So stick with me, and let's go get your power back.

KEY TAKEAWAYS AND REFLECTIONS

You are only as strong *as you will let yourself be*. Your feelings are not imaginary, but you are also no longer a slave to them. We can look at our life without fear or regret and use what we find to change and grow into the person we have always envisioned ourselves to be. Everyone has a different story, but we who read this book all share the same uncommon pain: We continually place ourselves in a position to be hurt or unhappy or unfulfilled. We have decided that all of that has to stop, and now we know there is a solution. We will be heroic and brave in this undertaking because, at the end of the day, we can decide our own worth and assign value to our own heart, and going forward, we will refuse to let anyone else dictate our reality.

Because that's not our crap; *that's their crap*. So, you know what? *We can let them have it back*. We don't have to own that stuff anymore, because it isn't ours.

Moving forward, we will listen exclusively to that voice inside of *us* that wants us to be happy and healthy and free.

When she was alive, Maya Angelou gave us an axiom to live by, if not to live up to. She taught us that courage is the most important of all the virtues, because without courage you can't practice any other virtue consistently. You can practice any virtue erratically, but none consistently without courage. It takes courage to trust. It takes courage to love. It takes courage to be kind, or to be patient, or to be fair. *Especially with yourself.*

Let's be courageous together.

CHAPTER TWO

Start Your Road to Recovery

Living in recovery is not a cakewalk. You already know this because you are reading this book. Perhaps you've tried to alter the course of your love life and failed or, even worse, become ensconced in a relationship where none of your needs are valued. Or you've found yourself neglected or even abused, and you're wondering, "Why am I living this awful life trying to earn the love and affection of someone who couldn't give a rat's ass about me? What is it about me that compels me to leap from one horrible partner to the next or keeps me crushing on people who don't even know I'm alive? Why does this keep happening to me? Am I broken? Am I destined to forever be unhappy?"

Let me answer that one for you: NO.

WHAT DOES LOVE ADDICTION RECOVERY LOOK LIKE?

Once the love addict makes the decision to change their life, they cease being a victim and start living in recovery. That's what therapy is all about. Later, once you've identified what motivates you to become entangled in toxic, painful relationships (real or imagined), your ability to pick and choose partners who will adore you and respond to your needs will *seem* effortless, but you and I will know it will have all been because you rolled up your sleeves and did the work. You got your power back.

In the beginning, it's all about vital introspection. Sometimes that means delving deep into our past to figure out what particular configuration of experiences contributed to our believing that living in anguish was our comfort zone.

Pain, suffering, and anguish are our enemies, and our addiction has somehow convinced us that they are the norm. That inner voice that guides us—that Beast—somehow wants us to be alone when the truth of the matter is, *we don't need to be.* My Beast used to inform most of the decisions I made; it was like a professional chess player, always thinking three or four moves ahead, so I never realized I was painting myself into a corner *with my own actions.* I cannot tell you how many times I've found myself heartbroken and alone because I followed the same trail of emotional bread crumbs over and over again.

We need to accept that our best thinking isn't what motivates us or makes our decisions; sometimes a clockwork of emotional scars dictates our behavior. When we know this, we can remain vigilant against these behaviors and take actions that yield the kinds of outcomes that lead to healthy, fulfilling relationships. We can acknowledge that we *deserve* to be in relationships with people who not only see us but adore us, so our feelings are appropriately reciprocated.

You'd be amazed by how many times I've watched a movie with friends and listened to them mock the lead characters. "Why doesn't she just dump him?!" they exclaim, or "He should just stand up for himself and leave!" All the while, I know that these very people sitting with me are themselves in painful, unrequited relationships, because they lack the ability to see how their behavior has *them* trapped.

Although we need to learn in order to recover, living in recovery has less to do with what we learn than what we do.

For me, when I'd decided that I didn't like the feelings I was having and was ready to do something about it, I was scared. I was still in college, working toward my master's, and I was suddenly thrust into a "physician, heal thyself" situation. I had all of the evidence laid out in front of me, yet my own actions had led me to misery time and time again! With this knowledge, I was confronted with the horrible possibility that maybe, in addition to being a love addict, I was also addicted to *shame*. I mean, why else would I keep doing things that made me feel bad about myself?

I found that there is nothing as excruciating as wandering the earth feeling unlovable or believing that if only I could earn someone's love, suddenly their attention or approval would validate me. I really needed to find a way to feel good about myself without help or hookups.

I needed to do a deep dive and figure out why I needed someone else to like me *for* me, because left to my own devices, *I was incapable of liking myself.* But that meant doing the work: *It meant amending my behavior so I took actions that made me feel good about myself,* which isn't always an easy thing to do—especially when determining what those actions should be.

Once you determine the right course of action, love addiction recovery is about committing to take the action, even when it looks silly or hard.

Our next two exercises are journaling exercises. For this to work, it's important to slow your thinking to the speed of a pen. Don't open your laptop and type these out; I want you to really cut through the muck and write what matters. Understand that there may not be enough space in the following pages to get it all out, and that's okay. You can always use a notebook or legal pad with this workbook. But it is critical to begin each exercise with the tasks outlined here, because we are going to circle back to a few of these exercises later in the book, and each new revelation will shed a different light on what you've written.

Lastly, remember that this is very personal work, and no one will see it but you. Let that help you be as honest and thorough as possible. If you find yourself having intense feelings about what you are writing, please take a break and have those feelings. Some of you may get angry when doing this work; others may cry. All of it is okay, but I don't want you to plow through those feelings. We can be kind to ourselves and not judge ourselves or our feelings.

None of this is our fault. We have been living in addiction, and that addiction has informed our behavior. But today we are Living in Recovery. And Living in Recovery means that we can look at the person we used to be, *take what we need from that person in order to grow,* and then move on.

Deep Dive

CHILDHOOD'S END

In looking back over your life, what childhood memories are:

a. Shameful
b. Dirty
c. Marked by rejection

a. ....
....
....
....
....
....
....

b. ....
....
....
....
....

c. ....
....
....
....
....

Deep Dive
MATCHMAKER, MAKE ME A MATCH

This exercise has three parts. Each part requires a moment of deep introspection; I encourage you to meditate on each assignment before committing pen to paper.

For the first part, I'd like you to go back in time and really look at yourself and how you were before you started dating or imagined yourself as part of a couple. This may mean going back to your preteen years. You can go back as far as the age of six if you want to; you decide.

Once you pick an age, write about that child. Tell me everything you remember about them. How did they look? What did they like? What were they like? I really want to know who this tiny person was and what made them happy. Did they have dreams and aspirations yet? What did they want out of life every day? Were they smart? Funny? Lonely? How did they feel about their parents? Their teachers? Their friends? Help me really see them and know them so that, if they were in a crowd, I'd know them right away.

1. **As I go back in time, I remember these things about myself:**

....

....

....

....

....

....

....

....

....

....

For the second part, I'd like you to focus on every meaningful relationship you've ever had and write every nice sentence you can remember that someone has spoken aloud to you. Try to be as specific as possible. Include your parents and teachers and friends and romantic interests. Try to remember the exact phrasing, if you can. "You're the best!" can easily be confused with "I think you're the best cook I know!" Try to limit what you write to positive things that were actually said *about* you, *to* you.

2. **People have said these things about me, to me:**

....

....

....

....

....

....

....

....

....

....

....

....

....

....

....

Lastly, let's look at what the people we've chosen to love romantically have said about us. Even our secret crushes. Dig deep in this part of the exercise—you need to write it all. Did your partner say you were a terrific dancer? Did your secret crush say you were stupid? Did your partner say you could stand to go to the gym more often? What kinds of criticisms do you remember actually hearing, and how did they make you feel in that moment? When they said they loved you, was it spontaneous and organic, or did they say it only after you'd done something for them or had sex with them? Did they ever compliment you? Did they ever point something out about you that they absolutely loved about you? Did they ever say something hateful or hurtful, regardless of whether or not they backpedaled later and apologized? Meditate long and hard on what you've heard from the people you chose to love, and write those statements down.

3. Things my lovers have said to me:

....

....

....

....

....

....

....

....

....

....

....

....

....

SETTING GOALS

As you work through this book, you will glean language that you can use to communicate your needs better. You will also learn how to identify your feelings and the precipitating events that trigger them. Typically, we are triggered by external situations and circumstances. A fire in the kitchen while cooking will trigger fear, which will motivate us to desperately seek out a fire extinguisher.

Conversely, someone pulling away from us will trigger a built-in response or knee-jerk reaction that may have been encoded into our psyche when we were children. An example of how that might have looked: When she felt like it, Mommy tickled us and told us she loved us. But that lasted only three minutes. The rest of the day, she was on the phone with her friends complaining about how trapped she felt or how miserable she was having to stay home and watch us, or she sent us to our room to play with our toys while she watched soap operas, or she left us playing in the backyard each day while she did the dishes or cleaned the house. All of this sent a very real message to our childhood selves. It told us that people who love or care about us, ignore us.

If we had an abusive parent who hit us or verbally attacked us, seemingly without provocation, our childhood showed us that volatile, abusive partners were the people who loved us. So, naturally we are going to devote our resources to seeking replacements for those people rather than setting new and better goals for ourselves.

Here are some examples of the goals I set for myself in my recovery:

My Goal for Today: Understand that how someone demonstrates love for me will usually have nothing to do with me. I am the person who needs to stop showing up for relationships where I am not appreciated or adored.

My Goal for Tomorrow: Stop gravitating toward and attaching myself to people who either behave badly (verbally or even physically abuse me, cheat on me, or repeatedly abandon me) or who are emotionally distant or unavailable. This is important because if I were to perform an autopsy on a toxic relationship, I would easily see how I was the one who put myself in a position to be hurt. But for now, I can simply choose to walk away from the people who are sources of anguish in my life.

My Goal for the Future: Don't expect anyone to do for me what I will not do for myself, which is love myself. I will do the work and discover who I am and find within myself the ability to love who I am, so I can take care of myself emotionally and find a partner I can truly trust and adore.

We need to be realistic about our goals, if only because we need to have successful hurdles to cross. We don't want to set ourselves up for failure, which happens when we set unrealistic goals. By realistic, I mean goals that are attainable by doing the work. No gymnast does a backflip perfectly the first time. In this instance, doing the work means honoring the goals you set for yourself while accepting that *it has to be earned.*

Deep Dive

THREE GOALS

Everyone has their own definition of what a healthy love life looks like—we'll set those beliefs aside for now and revisit them later in this workbook. Let's instead focus on the behaviors that make us unhappy in this particular area of our life. What behaviors—things you're doing—are constantly placing you in a position to be hurt? *Really examine that question.*

   Now list three goals that will put you on the other side of those behaviors. For example, if you were a drug addict, you would write something like:

GOAL #1: Stop using drugs and figure out how to not relapse anymore.

Take a deep breath and reflect: What do *you* hope to achieve by doing the work?

GOAL #1:

....

....

....

GOAL #2:

....

....

....

GOAL #3:

....

....

....

YOUR LOVE ADDICTION RECOVERY PLAN

We've talked about goals and the importance of baby steps as we approach the milestones in our recovery, so it's time to talk about putting together a comprehensive plan for recovery. This plan needs to be loose and forgiving but also specific to your individual needs. I can help you come up with a plan and give you strategies, but it'll be on *you* to actually fight the battles and move the stones. So remember this in all things: You are only as strong as you will *LET* yourself be.

In putting together your love addiction recovery plan, we'll lock it down with four concise steps:

1. Identify what your specific addiction issue looks like.

2. Set some recovery goals.

3. Commit to specific actions you will take.

4. Develop a support system.

First, you are going to state, unequivocally, WHAT YOUR SPECIFIC ADDICTION ISSUE LOOKS LIKE with regard to attachment. First identified by English psychologist John Bowlby, attachment theory suggests that there are three types or paradigms of attachment to others that can be identified by your propensity to align with one of three definitive statements:

1. **SECURE ATTACHMENT** (whereby love and trust come easily): "It is easy for me to trust others and get close to them. I do not live in fear of being hurt or betrayed. I always feel connected to others and enjoy sharing new experiences with them."

2. **ANXIOUS ATTACHMENT** (whereby one longs to be intimate with others but is continuously scared of being let down and often precipitates crisis in relationships through counterproductively aggressive behavior): "I find that closeness is a difficult and arduous process. I doubt the validity and sincerity of relationships. To compensate, I become clingy, jealous, and untrusting, which tends to push people away."

3. **AVOIDANT ATTACHMENT** (whereby it feels much easier to avoid the dangers of intimacy through emotional anorexia): "In relationships, I am uncomfortable with intimacy and often do not know who I should pity more: Them for wanting to be closer to me, or myself for allowing it."

The love addict will typically belong to either the avoidant or the anxious camp. Figuring out which group we belong to allows us to arm ourselves with the specific knowledge we will need to develop healthy long-term relationships.

It's important to mention that love addicts with avoidant or anxious attachment issues will tend to find, gravitate toward, and fall in love with someone from the other group—that is, a person with avoidant issues tends to be attracted to a person with anxious attachment issues, and vice versa. Making these relationships work often requires vigilance and sensitivity (we'll talk more about this later).

Once we've figured out the attachment style, we can SET SOME RECOVERY GOALS, which will help identify our roles in the problem and, for lack of a better term, *cut those wires* (thus starving the problem of our participation). Our goals should be broad in order to replace dysfunctional behaviors with healthier ones that yield positive consequences.

After the goals are set, we can then COMMIT TO ACTIONS THAT WE WILL TAKE. Notice that I did not say "*can* take." Once we commit to taking an action, we *have* to take it so we can process the result of the action and grow. Imagine there are three frogs on a log. One frog decides to jump off the log. How many frogs are left? Three. *Because deciding to do something and actually doing it are two entirely different things.*

The same holds true for your love addiction recovery plan. The language we use when outlining these actions will be specific and nonnegotiable, so great care must be taken when crafting them to mean what you say. Actions will always have deadlines. For example, *I will "unfollow" all of his or her social media accounts by Friday, October 4* has both an action and a deadline. If this sounds strict and inflexible, just remember, everyone will determine their own action steps.

Finally, you will be asked to DEVELOP A SUPPORT SYSTEM comprised of a person or persons who will intervene in unhelpful behavior when you self-report it:

LOVE ADDICT: I'm going to that coffee shop on Third Street. Would you like me to get you anything?

SUPPORT PERSON: Isn't that where so-and-so works? I thought you told me seeing them made you feel bad about yourself. Why don't you go to the one on Hauser?

Choose your accountabili-buddies wisely, as they will always step up and help redirect you away from the source of your anguish. *Committing contrary actions will help you grow new neural pathways and diminish the power and intensity of the old ones.* Sometimes you might need help determining what those actions *are.*

Deep Dive
DEFINE YOUR ATTACHMENT

Carefully study the three attachment paradigms (page 34) and discern which one best describes you. Justify your selection by writing about your interactions with a past partner that support your choice. Be as honest as possible to be thorough. Be heroic in this essay and write it all out; you are the only person who will ever read this.

In reflecting on my past relationships, it's clear that I am:

- ☐ ANXIOUS
- ☐ AVOIDANT
- ☐ SECURE

And I feel this is my truth because:

....

....

....

....

....

....

....

....

....

Deep Dive
BABY STEPS

Action steps are the things only you can do to move toward a healthier life. For me, my first action was "build a support system," mostly because I lived in so much shame about my love life, I didn't think I'd ever have the courage to ask for help. But I did. *And I'm glad I did.*

What actions do you think would help you achieve your goals? Let's figure out three that you can take and attach deadlines to them. We can revisit this table and check them off later, when they're done. Be sure to choose realistic deadlines; you don't want to set yourself up to fail. Respect the process and understand that this is harder than it seems—that's why this exercise is called Baby Steps. Give yourself a wide berth.

ACTION	DEADLINE

PHILLIP'S DILEMMA,
PART 1

Phillip identifies as an AVOIDANT type and finds himself constantly getting into relationships with ANXIOUS ATTACHMENT types. He is a handsome man who boasts of being the ultimate bumblebee, flying from flower to flower and never staying in any one place for too long. But secretly, Phillip longs for true connection. A self-labeled hopeless romantic, Phillip cries at sad movies and roots for the good guy to get the girl. His iPad is full of romantic comedies, but his iPhone is full of numbers of people he will never call a second time. Master of the one-night stand, Phillip finds himself going to bed alone more and more nowadays and wants nothing more than to find a true partner and someday start a family.

The people he dates are always so clingy, though, because they're ANXIOUS. He's uncomfortable with public displays of affection—even holding hands across a restaurant table can feel like nails on a blackboard to his avoidant heart. He'll do it if he thinks sex is the payoff, but he never initiates public intimacy; he merely tolerates it until he gets what he wants: a warm body in his bed, someone he can laugh with and eat take-out Chinese food with while watching the movies he loves so much.

But when the sun comes up, Phillip's actions ensure that his partners depart, and he cannot seem to help himself in this department, no matter how much he longs for a long-term relationship.

The work for Phillip is to recognize when he is committing what we call *old behaviors*. These are recurring behaviors that always yield the same result: Phillip is left alone and unfulfilled. He needs to recognize when his ANXIOUS partner is initiating closeness and respond in a way that promotes that closeness, so that he himself feels like a partner who is pulling his own weight in the relationship instead of the bad guy who is constantly accused of leading people on.

(CONTINUED)

The stranger he brought home represents the potential for a long-term relationship, and Phillip has to amend his own behavior in order to overcome his own latent fear of what he really wants and achieve it.

Phillip also needs to communicate his need for emotional independence in a way that is sensitive to his new partner's need for closeness. Phillip has to adopt a "fake it 'til you make it" attitude in the beginning as he trudges through this new, uncharted territory. He needs to observe the moments where he sabotages the relationship due to defense mechanisms he developed at a young age, when he found it safer to remove himself from the equation to protect himself from repeated disappointment or pain.

Although he is an adult, Phillip still needs to *grow all the way up* and individuate himself from his childhood traumas, and *reparent* himself so he can be happy. He needs to acknowledge that his new partner *wants* him and *wants to make him happy* and that they have come into the relationship with a veritable constellation of attachment needs that, in the beginning, may have seemed overwhelming to Phillip but are on the whole pretty common.

In layman's terms? In order to get what he wants out of life, *Phillip may need to get over his past hang-ups and do the work.*

KEY TAKEAWAYS AND REFLECTIONS

We all have attachment issues, all of which were born of experiences we had while growing up. None of these issues are inherently good or bad, but love addiction can take our attachment issues to the extreme and leave us unable to reach or fulfill our goals.

Thankfully, the love addict's recovery plan takes into account these idiosyncrasies and gives us a plan of action to remedy them, one by one, by first identifying our goals and then committing the actions necessary to meet them.

Until now, our own emotional vocabulary has been limited to words like *want, need, pain, rejection,* and *abandonment.* But now we have an opportunity to open the cathedral doors to a whole new world of emotional intelligence—one that will allow us to tweak the mechanisms we put in place and free us to experience new and sometimes frightening levels of love.

True, it goes against the grain of what you've been doing your entire life until now. But that doesn't mean that the love you deserve won't be just as good or better than the love you fantasize about!

CHAPTER THREE

Identify Your Beliefs

I love animals, and I hate to see one getting abused. Take the circus elephant, for example. In the circus, when a mother is taken away from her calf to go perform in the big top, the tiny elephant experiences a separation anxiety that knows no bounds. It squeals and cries out for its mother, and it usually takes many strong men to contain the animal as its mother is led away. One end of a large, heavy chain is looped around the baby elephant's ankle, and the other is fastened to a large metal spike that is driven into the ground. The baby elephant tries and tries to break the chain, but it cannot, and eventually the exhausted baby elephant simply gives up.

The baby elephant is always reunited with its mother, but the baby elephant doesn't catch on. Time and time again, it struggles against the heavy iron chain until it learns to give up. This is why, when you go to the circus, you will often see massive, powerful elephants being held in place by a flimsy cord of rope and a shoddy wooden peg: The elephant has learned to give up the moment it feels the resistant tug on its ankle. It has no idea that as an adult, it could smash through anything that stood in its way and drag the circus tent along with it!

Well, you know what? *People are the same way.* As children, we adopt little "elephant beliefs" that no longer serve us in adulthood, and we tend to recycle them over and over and over again.

BELIEFS AND DISTORTED THINKING

I was born in 1952, which means that I was raised in an era when the school systems had no diagnostic tools for the early recognition of learning disabilities. Like many others of this age group can probably relate to, my dyslexia went undiagnosed for decades. I lacked the ability to read fluently, mostly because—for reasons unknown to me at the time—words just got jumbled up in my head. I couldn't keep up with the other kids, and my grades suffered, as did my need for recognition from my family and friends. It was a nightmare because *I grew up thinking I was stupid.*

I know today that I am not stupid. I'm actually kind of okay, intellectually. I've learned all about my affliction and, while doing so, overcame it and went back to school and earned my master's in psychology. I'm not telling you this because I want to brag or boast; I'm telling you this because for the longest time, *I told myself that I was stupid.* To say that I lived the first half of my life with a deep, dark secret is a misnomer: I was traumatized. That trauma informed not only my view of the world but also how I viewed myself as a person. Over and over again, like torture, my own mind told me that I was stupid and that I couldn't and wouldn't amount to anything.

I think some of you do that same thing. Maybe you're not telling yourself you're stupid specifically. But I've been around long enough to know that the mind can be like a bad neighborhood—*you don't want to go in there alone.* There are giant neon signs in our mind that flash negative messages over and over again, and these messages inform how we see ourselves and how we relate to the world. We call these *cognitive distortions*, or in the words of SNL's Al Franken, "stinkin' thinkin'":

"He's late. He's probably with another woman."
"I'm alone because I am ugly."
"She doesn't like me; she's just too chicken to dump me."
"I'm worthless."
"My mother has always been ashamed of me."
"My friends laugh about me behind my back."

Cognitive distortions are beliefs that have no grounding in the truth, but like the flimsy rope around the elephant's ankle, they hold us hostage and rob us of our power.

In the 1960s, psychiatrist Aaron Beck pioneered research on cognitive distortions, which led to a treatment method known as cognitive behavioral therapy (CBT) as well as the identification of several patterns of distorted thinking:

Polarized thinking is a form of thinking that places everything into black-and-white extremes. It's the thinking that tells us that when we fail a math test, we will never be good at math, and we should give up and drop out of school and simply give up on life. It's also the kind of thinking that says we are destined to be discovered washing dishes in a diner and given a record contract without ever having a singing lesson.

Personalization is an insidious one for love addicts, because this thinking tells us repeatedly that it is all about us. If our partners are having a bad day, we secretly believe they are mad at us. If our parents alter a routine, we tell ourselves it's because they want to avoid us. We assume the blame for circumstances beyond our control and often feel persecuted or intentionally excluded.

Emotional reasoning is the belief that our emotions are an authority on whatever is happening in reality. It is the thinking that says if we suspect our partner of cheating, then they must be cheating, despite all evidence to the contrary. And while our feelings may not be imaginary, historically we know that they aren't always right: *Feelings aren't facts.*

Labeling is a cognitive distortion that reduces the world around us or even ourselves to its simplest components, usually with negative descriptors like *drug addict* or *cripple*. Labeling can diminish our self-esteem in an instant or cause us to underestimate our colleagues or peers.

Catastrophizing leads us to live and operate in a world where worst-case scenarios rule:

She isn't home on time? She might be dead in an alley or, worse, in the arms of another man.

Is that a sneeze or a cough? Maybe I have cancer!

Overgeneralization has been associated with post-traumatic stress disorder (PTSD) and usually involves reaching a conclusion about many things based on one single event or outcome. Did you get a divorce? Your head may tell you that *you're just horrible at relationships and you'll never love again.*

Each of us has a voice in our mind that tells us who we are. It takes a lot of introspection to determine whose voice is in your head. For some, it's an overbearing mother, for others a doting father, wise schoolteacher, or taunting older sibling—but the voice is real.

It's the voice that exclaims, *"You idiot!"* when you knock something off a table or sign the wrong date on a cashier's check. It's also the voice that says, *"Who am I kidding? Nobody will ever truly love me; there's too much wrong with me."* Have you ever heard the phrase *"If anyone ever talked to me the way I talk to myself, I'd punch 'em in the mouth!"*?

Deep Dive
RECORD YOUR PROBLEMATIC THOUGHTS

This checklist is excerpted from Sharon L. Johnson's *Therapist's Guide to Clinical Intervention.* We've touched on a few of these patterns, but I'd like you to look them over again and personally assess which types of cognitive distortions best apply to you. Read the type of distortion, ruminate on it for a moment—really examine it—and then place a check mark in the corresponding box if you think that particular line of thinking applies to you.

Then, reflect on and write about an instance that serves as an example of your own cognitive distortion.

☐ **Filtering:** You take the negative details of a situation and magnify them while filtering out all positive aspects.

....

....

....

....

....

☐ **Polarized thinking:** Things are black or white, good or bad. You have to be perfect or you're a failure. There is no middle ground; it's all or nothing.

....

....

....

....

....

☐ **Overgeneralization:** This is coming to a general conclusion based on a single incident or piece of evidence. If something bad happens once, you expect it to happen over and over again.

....

....

....

....

....

☐ **Mind reading:** Without them saying so, you think you know what people are feeling and why they act the way they do. In particular, you are able to tell how people are feeling toward you—and it's usually negative.

....

....

....

....

....

☐ **Catastrophizing:** You expect disaster. You notice or hear about a problem and start obsessing over "what-ifs." What if tragedy strikes? What if it happens to you?

....

....

....

....

....

☐ **Personalization:** This is thinking that everything people do or say is some kind of reaction to you. You also compare yourself to others, trying to determine who's smarter, better looking, etc.

....

....

....

....

....

☐ **Control fallacies:** If you feel *externally controlled*, you see yourself as helpless, a victim of fate. The fallacy of *internal control* means you feel responsible for the pain and happiness of everyone around you.

....

....

....

....

....

☐ **Fallacy of fairness:** You feel resentful because you think you know what's fair but other people won't agree with you.

....

....

....

....

....

☐ **Blaming:** You hold others responsible for your pain. Or, conversely, you blame yourself for every problem or reversal of fortune without regard to external causes.

....

....

....

....

....

☐ **Shoulds:** You have a list of ironclad rules about how you and other people should act. People who break the rules anger you, and you feel guilty if you violate the rules.

....

....

....

....

....

☐ **Emotional reasoning:** You believe that what you feel must be true. If you feel stupid and boring, then you must be stupid and boring.

....

....

....

....

....

☐ **Fallacy of change:** You expect that other people will change to suit you if you just pressure or cajole them enough. You need to change people because your hopes for happiness seem to depend entirely on them.

....

....

....

....

....

☐ **Global labeling:** You generalize one or two qualities into a negative global judgment.

....

....

....

....

....

☐ **Being right:** You are continually on trial to prove that your opinions and actions are correct. Being wrong is unthinkable, and you will go to any lengths to demonstrate your rightness.

....

....

....

....

....

☐ **Heaven's reward fallacy:** You expect all your sacrifice and self-denial to pay off, as if there were someone keeping score. You feel bitter when the reward doesn't come.

....

....

....

....

....

Deep Dive
IDENTIFY YOUR PROBLEMATIC
LOVE THOUGHTS

Daily affirmations aren't just a punch line in some skit on a comedy show. For many people, they are a path to real emotional recovery. They are truly your self-esteem's first line of defense against the very real threat of cognitive distortion, and they are a practice I recommend adopting immediately. As we get deeper and deeper into this thing, you will need to know exactly who you are and exactly what you're capable of, and I'm willing to bet that you had no idea who or what that was when you picked up this book. So walk with me, talk with me, **and let's separate the horse crap from the ice cream**.

In looking back over your life, what were your ideas about your love life? What were you expecting? What did you imagine being in a relationship would look like? What influenced you? Was it movies, books, television, something else? Was it what you saw or experienced in your parents' relationship? Or a relative's? Write about what you envisioned for yourself while growing up and why.

....

....

....

....

....

....

....

....

....

Deep Dive
NEON SIGNS

Like it or not, our negative thinking dictates our day-to-day reality in a very profound way. Some of it is so ingrained that even with this exercise, you may not catch it.

So, I am inviting you to take some time and really reflect before entering the types of thinking we are going to be isolating. Live a bit of your life and pay attention to what your head is telling you, and then write it down so you can tangibly look at how you treat yourself on a daily basis.

It's a pretty simple exercise, but I'll admit it can be harrowing. You don't have to get it all in one go. Negative thoughts are like neon signs, remember? They just keep flashing the same message over and over again.

IN LOOKING BACK OVER YOUR LIFE, WHAT NEGATIVE IDEAS DO YOU FIND YOURSELF CONSTANTLY REINFORCING IN YOUR MIND?

Example: *This person will never go for someone like me.*

1. ....

....

....

2. ....

....

....

3. ....

....

....

4. ....

....

....

5. ....

....

....

6. ....

....

....

7. ....

....

....

8. ....

....

....

9. ....

....

....

10. ....

....

....

11.
....

....

....

12.
....

....

....

13.
....

....

....

14.
....

....

....

15.
....

....

....

THE THINGS WE THINK BUT DO NOT SAY

The pendulum swings both ways in affairs of the mind and heart, and this next exercise should reflect that nicely.

In looking back over your life, what **good** discoveries have you made about yourself? If the neon jungle is flashing all the negative aspects of who you are, let's try to make a list of all of the good things you believe about yourself. Dig deep, and be as honest as possible to be thorough. What do you like about yourself? What do you love about yourself? What are you most proud of?

....

....

....

....

....

....

....

....

....

....

....

....

....

....

....

THE GHOST OF CHRISTMAS PAST

Before we move forward, I feel that we should take a detour into the realm of forgiveness. In that regard, this next exercise is important. Because I want you to forgive yourself.

I'd like you to choose a time when you are utterly alone and find a mirror (your bathroom mirror will do just fine). I'd like you to really look at yourself. Look at all the things that make you, well . . . *you.*

And then I want you to try to forgive yourself for whatever comes to mind, one thing at a time, and explain why you did what you did.

"I'm sorry we got mixed up with Jack. It was my job to take care of you, and I put us in that awful man's house. He didn't treat you well at all, and that was all my fault and I'm sorry."

"I'm sorry I let you believe that she was the one even though we knew going in that she had issues with sex. My faithfulness was not a guarantee that she wouldn't cheat on us, and I let you believe that lie and we almost lost everything because of it. That was my fault and I'm sorry."

"I'm sorry I kept telling you that Paulie wasn't a bad man; he had just never met anyone like us and said that our love could change him. He hurt you, and that was my fault for staying as long as I did. I'm gonna do right by you, but for now, you need to know that I am so sorry."

You get the gist. Let it all out—relationship after relationship, failed encounter after failed encounter. Try to own as much of your behavior as possible. It's painful, I know, but we are going to take harder looks, and now is the time to develop the ego strength to withstand the tasks ahead, *and it all starts by forgiving yourself*.

Some of you might find this is more effective if done in writing; in that case, go ahead and use your journal as your mirror.

Good luck. I am with you.

Deep Dive

SIFT THROUGH THE ASHES

Did you forgive yourself? How did you do? What feelings, if any, came up for you? What did you choose to forgive yourself for that impacted you the most? Did you have any revelations about your past relationships?

I understand that it may not all be fresh in your memory at this point, but *let's try to write down what we remember about the experience*. It's okay if you remember other instances while you are logging this experience below; you can go back to the mirror and apologize and forgive yourself for those also if you like.

Take your time with this. I'll always be right where you left me.

....

....

....

....

....

....

....

....

....

....

....

....

....

....

....

....

JEANETTE'S DILEMMA

Jeanette's first date with Robby was a success! They met at a nightclub when she was pretty drunk. They kissed for a while, until her friends told her the club was closing and it was time to go. Robby was the perfect gentleman and gave her his number, asking her to call him so he could take her out. However, when she called, he didn't exactly remember who she was. Still, he was charming and made good on his word and took Jeanette out to dinner. He didn't like the dress she was wearing and criticized her dinner choices off the menu, but he made her laugh, and she was still very attracted to him. After dinner, as they were walking to their cars, Jeanette marveled at how handsome he was and felt like the luckiest girl alive. Robby invited her to follow him back to his place, but she had to be at work early the next morning, so they kissed in the parking lot, and he promised he'd call her and take her out that weekend. He also commented that maybe she shouldn't wear lipstick next time because he didn't like how it looked on her (which was confusing because it was the same lipstick she'd been wearing the night they met). Jeanette got home and kicked off her shoes and flopped onto her bed in a giddy whirl, thinking, *I've met a man, and he is perfect, and he likes me, and all I have to do is remember the food he likes for me to order and stop wearing lipstick! Oh, and get rid of the dress. Robby didn't like the dress. . . .*

CHANGE YOUR BELIEFS

In this chapter, we've explored the different ways our beliefs shape who and what we accept ourselves to be, but we haven't brushed upon what we should do if we don't like who and what this person is. We haven't talked about how to overwrite our thinking and change our beliefs to more accurately reflect our true, authentic selves.

I want to say this is easy. You simply wake up one day and decide to be a certain way and then, *presto*, instant new you! But the human mind doesn't work that way. We are, all of us, a sophisticated collection of experiences that inform both our decisions and our narrative. These experiences touch and shape us, but not one of them can control us unless we let it. We are stronger than our stories because they don't have to define us and *because we have the power to rewrite them.*

It's scary, yes. Especially when the beliefs we have about ourselves are born from experiences we hardly remember, but it is possible to rewrite them if you work at it every day. What is important is that you fortify the efforts by linking them to real experiences. I'll show you how.

Not everybody's process is the same. But here are tried-and-true ways of changing what you believe about yourself and the world around you:

1. **Watch and adjust accordingly.** Now that you understand what your negative self-talk is, maintain a level of vigilance and begin to correct it. The next time you drop something and exclaim, "Man, I'm a clumsy idiot!" take a breath and remind yourself that no, you're just someone who dropped something—it happens all the time. Or, better yet (and this one's a hard one, believe me), the next time you forget something, don't smack yourself on the head and roll your eyes and go back to get it; just go back and get it. Because no one cares that you turned back around to get something you forgot. No one is judging you except yourself! Be kind to yourself. Life is too short to waste it reinforcing bad beliefs.

2. **Forgive yourself.** It sounds cheesy, I know, but self-forgiveness is the fastest way I know to embrace change and move into a space where loving yourself is possible. I humiliated myself in my past relationships, and I remember every minute. But my healing is born of the fact that I can remember it and talk about it *and not relive them over and over again.* I'm free, and you can be, too!

3. **Get in touch with "The Great I Am."** You have spent so much of your life living in the fantasy of who everyone told you to be; get on board with who you've always wanted to be. What is *that* person like? Is it someone who is constantly seeking validation or approval from others? I don't think so. The person you want to be is wholly emotionally self-sustaining; they just need to take some baby steps and walk into the light.

4. **Live in your truth.** Understand that the affirmations you will be coming up with in this workbook aren't contrived or patronizing—*they came from you.* No one wrote them for you. You did that! Do you have any idea how amazing you are? *It's okay to be amazing.*

5. **Carve new experiences.** Hack your neural pathways. Go for a walk in your neighborhood. I don't care if you live in Beverly Hills or South Central, get outside and take a walk around your block and let the sunlight fall on your face.

I take your emotional and mental health very seriously—it's my life's work, both professionally and personally. And I want this to work for you. I want you to experience the freedom that I have. Your addiction shouldn't get to choose your partner anymore. The delusion that this is and will always be your lot in life *has* to be smashed. Changing your beliefs is possible, *but it takes time and vigilance and effort.* And you're on your way.

THROUGH THE LOOKING GLASS

Let's start with a simple exercise to identify your core beliefs. It's going to be pretty simple, unlike our other exercises; you won't be investing too much thought into it. Just respond to the questions with whatever comes to mind without embellishing your answers.

1. If I had to be honest, I'd have to admit that I am:

   ....

   ....

   ....

   ....

   ....

2. When I think of other people, I think they are:

   ....

   ....

   ....

   ....

   ....

3. By and large, I feel as if life is:

   ....

   ....

   ....

   ....

   ....

Now examine those answers. Where or whom did they come from? Did any experiences help shape those responses? How do you feel about your responses? Take some time and journal your thoughts about your responses here:

....

....

....

....

....

....

....

....

....

....

....

....

....

....

....

....

....

....

Deep Dive
THE GREAT I AM

You may find a lot of daily affirmations online that will help shape both your burgeoning day and how you perceive yourself, but it's possible to be even more proactive about taking your power back. For this exercise, try to create your own affirmations by digging deep and completing the following sentences.

I am excited to ....

.... today.

My mind is ....

....

I am going to give 100 percent to ....

....

Today my life will ....

....

I have the willpower to ....

....

I am .... and can do whatever I set my mind to.

I am becoming the best version of myself at ....

....

I am excited and can't wait to ....

.... today.

I have a strong sense of ....

....

I am confident about ....

....

I am proud of myself for ....

....

Every day I am getting better at ....

....

I am motivated to ....

....

Policing my own negative self-talk is getting easier every day because I ....

....

....

....

DAILY AFFIRMATIONS

Upon waking each day, fold a daily affirmation into your morning ritual (while fixing a cup of coffee, showering, etc.). Make sure the affirmation is TRUE. You don't have to believe it (your Beast probably won't let you, not yet), but it should still be spoken aloud. You can use the affirmations you came up with in the previous exercise or use one of these:

1. My body is healthy; my mind is brilliant; my soul is tranquil.

2. I forgive those who have harmed me in my past and peacefully detach from them.

3. I am courageous and I stand up for myself.

4. I am a powerhouse; I am indestructible.

5. Many people look up to me and recognize my worth; I am admired.

After you speak your chosen affirmation, say this aloud:

"This is a truth about me that I myself have uncovered. I will protect this truth as if it were a newborn child. I will let nothing and no one attack or criticize this truth. Not even myself."

Doing this exercise shouldn't take more than five minutes out of your busy day, but the payoff will probably last a lifetime.

KEY TAKEAWAYS AND REFLECTIONS

Knowing your attachment style is important. I implore you to pay close attention to the attributes of your style so you can function in any relationship in a manner that serves *your* truth. This way, you no longer need to compromise who you are for love. This way, you don't have to spend every relationship begging for love, living in a fantasy of what might be, or sabotaging the things that might make you happy.

With what you've learned, you can bring more to the table than your addiction issues, and you can get more from your partner because the communication will be genuine, intelligent, and informed.

Like elephants, we learn things when we are very young that no longer serve us in adulthood, and it is time to cast those things aside. We can forgive ourselves for past mistakes and move forward into healing. We can also examine our own thinking and understand that while the heart wants what the heart wants, *we* are in control of our own destiny, and *we* decide what is best for us.

We don't ever have to be afraid to take chances and grow.

CHAPTER FOUR

Connect with Your Feelings

f Becky develops unrequited feelings of love for Joe (as she's done so many times for so many other men in the past), subconsciously she feels safe. She doesn't have to brave the uncharted waters of true intimacy. She never has to really get to know Joe, nor does she even have to risk rejection. *She is in control.* She is unhappy and unfulfilled, yes, but she is also the captain of her ship. Her feelings are constantly telling her that Joe is "the one" and that if he could see her for who she truly is, he would miraculously fall in love with her, and the two would live happily ever after.

The same holds true for Phil, who is pining away for Julia, a happily married woman. It is safe for him to believe he has love feelings for her because she will never leave her husband, and the fantasy that someday she will see him for who he truly is and leave her marriage is a fantasy that keeps him coming back for more.

UNDERSTANDING YOUR LOVE EMOTIONS

For some love addicts, it can be about perpetuating the fantasy, but for others, it can be about control. Both Becky and Phil are normal, healthy human beings with needs that have to be met and who have both found ways to have deep, meaningful relationships with partners who probably don't even know that they are alive. Looking back over their stories, you can see patterns emerging, mostly from the ways in which they reflexively indulge elaborate fantasies regarding the chosen objects of their affection instead of digging deep and asking the really hard questions: *Why do I feel this way about this stranger? What am I getting out of this "relationship" with someone who neither sees nor cares about me? Why am I so afraid to risk rejection and move on?*

The love addict possesses a complicated constellation of erupting emotions, each more intense than your average day-to-day emotional spectrum because each is fueled by fantasy. Keeping things "right-size" is challenging for the love addict because so much of what they're feeling seems to be channeled through their desperate desire to connect with another person—so much so that they will sacrifice anything to achieve that connection. A love addict will sacrifice their livelihood, their friendships, and their family, all in the name of being with someone who, for what- ever reason, cannot be there for them in any real way that matters. Every relationship the love addict falls into is riddled with the illusion of control and codependence despite the shackles, which are easily shattered. But first, the love addict needs to connect with their own feelings.

In the early days of my own love addiction, I acquired the ability to paint all of my red flags green. I was so emotionally disorganized, I tended to ignore every warning sign that even suggested that, here again, I was placing myself in a position to be hurt. I simply refused to acknowledge those feelings. I wanted what I wanted and was willing to sacrifice my integrity to get it. The tenets of my own basic self-care were thrown out the window because I wanted *her*, I needed *her*, I was in love with *her*, no one would ever love, know, or understand me better than *her*, so I invested everything that I had in *her*, and I lived in terror of *her* leaving me every time!

All of that could have been avoided if I'd stopped for a minute and listened to what my feelings were telling me. In her best-selling book

Liespotting, Pamela Meyer explains that "lying is a cooperative act" and further states that "a lie only has power if you, yourself, agree to believe the lie."

But what if the lie is coming from within? What if, in my addiction, I was lying to myself to perpetuate the fantasy that the person I was enamored with was the only one for me? Or the heinous lie that if that person didn't love me back, I was unlovable and doomed to remain alone for the rest of my days? Continuing to believe those lies would have left me bereft of all human connection and hopelessly alone. I never would have met my wife, and we, in turn, would never have had any children. I would have robbed myself of all the happiness I'd enjoyed in the 18 years we were married.

I would have robbed myself of my own life. But thankfully, I did the work.

As human beings, none of us want to be hurt. Ever. As children, we usually develop very sophisticated threat-assessment skills. We know, through the learned readings of subtle or even subconscious cues, when someone means to do us wrong. More often than not, we meet people, decide that they are safe, and go to work on earning their trust and friendship so both parties feel safe and secure and can move forward without issue.

But sometimes we invite chaos into our life when we could have avoided it. We didn't connect with our feelings, and so we put ourselves in a position to be hurt.

Connecting with our feelings is necessary because only then can we truly get our power back. Our intuition will serve us in ways that it never has before because we will have plugged into that part of ourselves that we created specifically for the task of taking care of us.

As we strive to become our genuine, authentic selves, we discover an ability to make healthy decisions based on our own needs, wants, and desires, instead of decisions that go against what our feelings are telling us. More importantly, we move away from decisions that are informed by trauma, fear, or neurosis. We gain true control of our love life, and we are able to activate our role in every relationship we have. We become whole again.

LABEL YOUR EMOTIONS

In the Steven Spielberg adaptation of Alice Walker's novel *The Color Purple*, Whoopi Goldberg portrays Celie, a Black woman trapped in a loveless marriage. The scope of the story encompasses so much more, but I am minimizing here to get to the meat of her character's arc, because it isn't until she learns how to read that Goldberg's character realizes the world is much bigger and broader than she ever imagined.

In a spirited montage, her sister teaches her how to read by placing labels on every item in the house, thereby helping her make sense out of the chaos she finds herself in. Whoopi's character learns to read and, in doing so, *evolves*.

The same evolution lies in wait for the love addict because so much of what the love addict experiences is cyclic and repetitive. And in order to break that cycle, we need to evolve also.

Once we learn to connect with our emotions, the next step is learning how to label them. Mostly, this helps us because a broader emotional vocabulary prevents us from "*languaging*" ourselves into misery; it creates a buffer between what we feel or experience and how we choose to react.

UCLA professor of psychology Matthew D. Lieberman discovered the benefits of labeling our feelings. He noticed increased activity in the part of the brain called the amygdala whenever we are feeling angry (this is the part of the brain that responds to fear by triggering biological responses to protect us from danger). But he further noted that once the angry feeling is labeled, there is a decreased response in the amygdala and increased activity in the right ventrolateral prefrontal cortex (the part of the brain associated with inhibiting behavior and processing emotions).

Frankly put, naming your emotions with any real specificity helps you calm down and become less reactionary. If that's too daunting a notion, try to simply do the math:

EMOTIONAL INTELLIGENCE + SELF-AWARENESS = SERENITY

None of this is easy to achieve. If hell is repetition, these next exercises are going to be torture, because they serve as a crash course in emotional labeling as we learn how to identify feelings that would normally take us from pillar to post on any given day.

But first, a cheat sheet for the newly indoctrinated!

FEELING WHEEL

Originally designed by Dr. Gloria Willcox, the Feeling Wheel has become somewhat of a cornerstone in my practice. It's vital for identifying specific emotions you are feeling at any given time so they can be unpacked and resolved. Take a moment and check it out.

In any given situation, we may initially feel angry or sad or bad. The object here is to use the root feeling and work your way out to the outer ring to identify the more specific feeling you may be experiencing. Of course, if a feeling in the inner ring is the appropriate one, then use that.

In your writing and reflections, try to refer to this wheel as often as possible so you can be accurate about what is really occurring in that moment. Bear in mind that this wheel is merely a *suggestion* of feelings; there are hundreds more out there, some more advanced than this one. Each wheel, however, was created in the spirit of helping us become more emotionally literate. Add or subtract words as you see fit, and feel free to explore new ways to improve your emotional vocabulary!

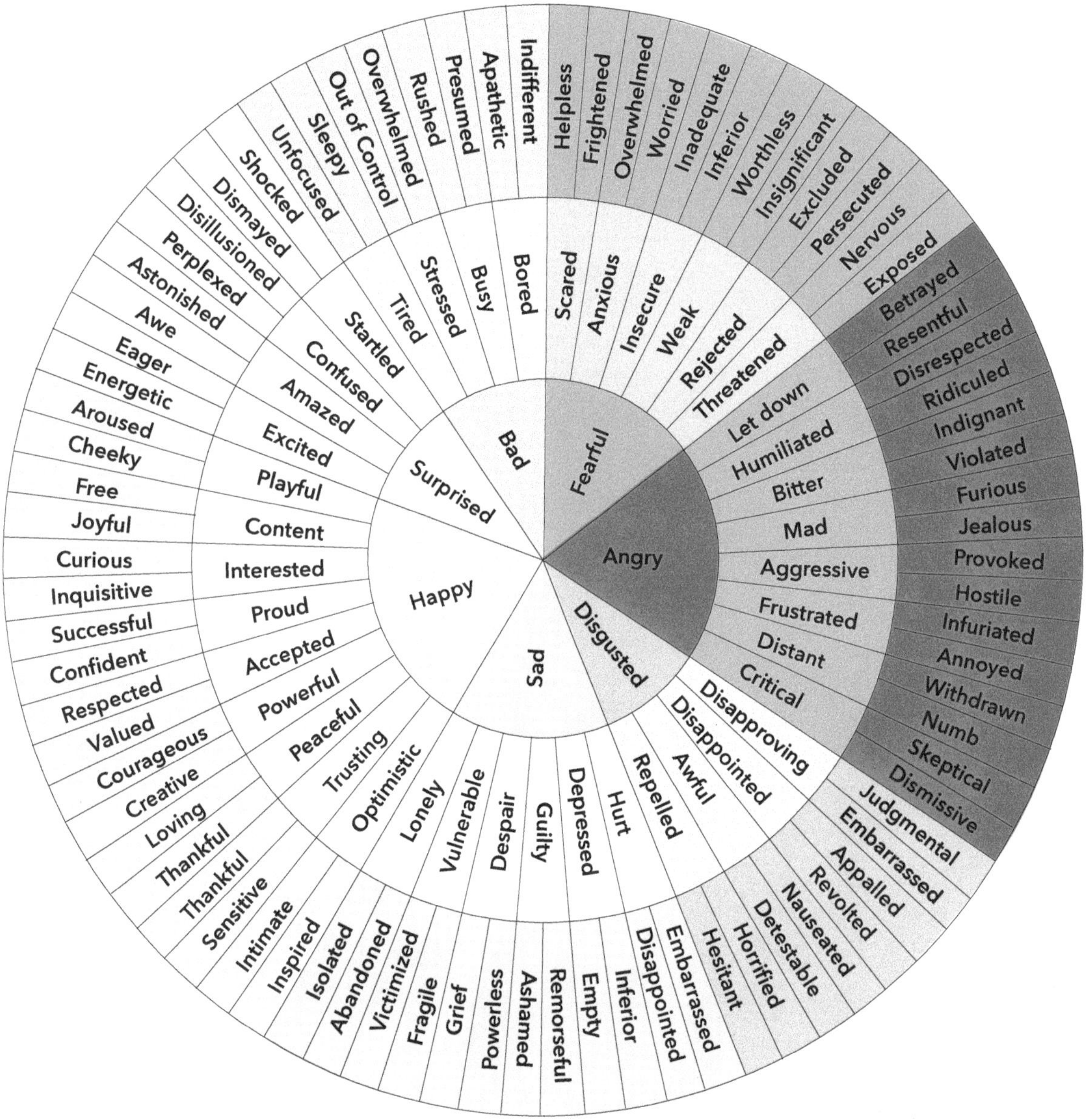

Happy
Surprised
Bad
Fearful
Angry
Disgusted
Sad
Playful
Content
Interested
Proud
Accepted
Powerful
Peaceful
Trusting
Optimistic
Free
Joyful
Curious
Inquisitive
Successful
Confident
Respected
Valued
Courageous
Creative
Loving
Thankful
Thankful
Sensitive
Intimate
Inspired
Hopeful
Cheeky
Aroused
Energetic
Eager
Awe
Astonished
Perplexed
Disillusioned
Dismayed
Shocked
Excited
Amazed
Confused
Startled
Tired
Stressed
Busy
Bored
Unfocused
Sleepy
Out of Control
Overwhelmed
Rushed
Presumed
Apathetic
Indifferent
Scared
Anxious
Insecure
Weak
Rejected
Threatened
Helpless
Frightened
Overwhelmed
Worried
Inadequate
Inferior
Worthless
Insignificant
Excluded
Persecuted
Nervous
Exposed
Let down
Humiliated
Bitter
Mad
Aggressive
Frustrated
Distant
Critical
Betrayed
Resentful
Disrespected
Ridiculed
Indignant
Violated
Furious
Jealous
Provoked
Hostile
Infuriated
Annoyed
Withdrawn
Numb
Skeptical
Dismissive
Disapproving
Disappointed
Awful
Repelled
Judgmental
Embarrassed
Appalled
Revolted
Nauseated
Detestable
Horrified
Hesitant
Hurt
Depressed
Guilty
Despair
Vulnerable
Lonely
Embarrassed
Disappointed
Inferior
Empty
Remorseful
Ashamed
Powerless
Grief
Fragile
Victimized
Abandoned
Isolated

Deep Dive

WHEEL . . . OF . . . FEELINGS!

Over the next several days, check in with yourself and identify what you are feeling. This can be done several times a day (recommended) or simply at night; it's up to you. Fill out the following table to the best of your ability. Pay attention to which feelings come up the most for you. In the beginning, I was surprised to see that anger was my go-to feeling when the truth was, more often than not, I'd simply had my feelings hurt or felt ashamed. When you are done with the exercise, highlight the feeling from the center of the circle that comes up for you the most, examine its chosen counterpart in the outer ring of the wheel, and then write about how that makes you feel. I've included an example to get you started:

INCIDENT	INITIAL FEELING	ACTUAL FEELING
The person I love did not call me today	Sad	Abandoned

YOUR EMOTIONAL TRIGGERS

When I watch a Super Bowl commercial and it makes me feel good, I am more apt to listen to the product's call to action and buy it. It doesn't matter what the product is (automobile, dishwashing liquid, candy bar, etc.); if I am emotionally triggered, I will act on those feelings and spend my hard-earned money on whatever they're selling. Can you relate?

The same holds true for real-life experiences, memories, or traumatic events: All of these inspire intense emotional reactions, regardless of what we are currently thinking or feeling, and almost always incite a reflexive action or outburst.

For the love addict with attachment issues, an avoidant partner may trigger a host of emotional responses, inspiring the addict's need to win them over at all costs, regardless of the consequence.

I first came across artist and mental health advocate Dominee Wyrick's graphic "What Triggered Me" while policing my teenage daughter's Instagram feed. Showcased on @BlessingManifesting, the graphic was inspired by a post Wyrick saw on social media from the Gottman Institute, which focuses on relationships. The graphic lists emotional triggers that compel people to respond in all sorts of uncharacteristically unhealthy ways. I've listed a variation of it here for you to use in this next exercise.

In looking over the list, can you write about what motivated you in your last unhealthy relationship? (I've listed an example in the first row; use as many rows as you need, or complete the exercise in your own journal if space is an issue.)

WHAT TRIGGERED ME

INCIDENT	I FELT	MY FEAR	ACTION
She didn't return my text messages quickly	Unloved, disrespected, powerless, frustrated, ignored, manipulated	I will be alone, I am not good enough, I am unlovable	Spend more money on her, snoop through her social media, overeat

MICHAEL'S DILEMMA

Michael initially came to me for help with substance abuse. A 28-year-old man with a single mother and two older sisters, Michael was raised in a household where women were constantly doting on him and were also the sole disciplinarians, oftentimes meting out physical punishment while reprimanding him. His primary male role model was a fly-by-night uncle whose chauvinistic ways masked a misogynist bent toward anything he considered effeminate or female. Michael lost his virginity at 16 to an older woman and states that the experience lent him a confidence that enabled him to pursue and bed women several years his senior for over a decade. He reports that he has never taken any of these women on as long-term partners and that what he wants more than anything is to meet and fall in love with a woman his own age, so he can marry and have children of his own.

He has begun to fantasize about a female coworker, claiming in one moment that he is "in love" with her and "obsessed" with her the next. Michael's best friend has grown frustrated with what he perceives as an inappropriate schoolboy's crush, and is astonished that such a sexually accomplished man continues to refuse to ask the coworker out on a date. Michael reports that he sometimes feels unattractive because he has proven himself incapable of connecting with a woman he truly desires and often wonders why this coworker keeps sending him mixed signals. Michael has not had sex with any other women since meeting her. Michael has identified that he needs to reevaluate what he really wants and then focus on taking the small but necessary steps to achieve his goals.

UNDERSTANDING EMOTIONAL REGULATION

We've talked about building an emotional vocabulary that will allow us to distance ourselves from reacting to external stimuli without processing them first. Many love addicts lack the impulse control necessary to resist putting themselves in a position to be hurt. Granted, some love addicts actively seek rejection (it helps perpetuate the narrative that they are broken and unlovable while simultaneously insulating them against having to be intimate with another human being), but many love addicts desperately want to be in healthy, fulfilling relationships. This conflict creates anguish and suffering.

The easiest way to demonstrate a lack of emotional regulation is to imagine someone who is high-strung and emotional. This person seems to have no filter or boundaries and is prone to angry outbursts over the tiniest things, or crying fits when simple solutions are readily available.

Being able to distance ourselves from self-imposed conflict or drama sounds good on paper, but exercising this tool kit in real time takes practice, mostly because many of our emotional responses are hardwired into our brain.

Self-regulation inserts a moment between feeling and reacting, affording us an opportunity to make a conscious decision about how we should proceed. This is not the same as stuffing our feelings. Suppressing feelings is never healthy; a healthier approach is to learn how to express them in a manner that serves our core values and reinforces our commitment to achieving our goals.

Imagine you're a race car driver and you're going 180 miles per hour. The landscape is whizzing by you, but you've done this before, so you know in a flash when to downshift while braking into a turn and when to make subtle adjustments to how you steer. With time and practice, you should be able to regulate your feelings in much the same way: with lightning-fast precision.

The key to achieving this goal lies in knowing what to do and when to do it. We have scores of significant feelings every day. How we deal with and express those feelings can be broken down into three choices:

1. We can take an action that is triggered by our emotions.

2. We can practice "restraint of pen and tongue" and not commit an action triggered by our emotions.

3. We can regulate the emotions that have been triggered by our emotions.

Option 3 is the best route to go. In the beginning, when I argued with the woman who would one day be my wife, I was careless in my anger and said hurtful things that I regretted the moment I said them. That was me living in option 1.

Eventually, I learned not to say hurtful things, but more often than not, I found myself suppressing my feelings, and eventually they came out anyway in some form or another, usually at inopportune moments. Option 2 didn't serve me, either. It rendered me passive-aggressive, and I wound up pushing her away.

However, once I started regulating my emotions, our quarrels took a dramatically different turn. I would say things like, "I'm really angry right now, but I love you, so let's table this until I've had a chance to cool down and collect my thoughts." This statement conveyed vital pieces of information to her, and it gave us a much-needed break from arguing. Even before storming out of our apartment, I was careful to say something like, "I'm going for a walk. I'll be back in an hour." This way, I was careful not to activate her abandonment issues. She knew where I was going and when I'd return.

Our marriage lasted 18 years, mostly because we'd both learned how to communicate our feelings with one another without having our feelings dictate our behavior.

As a love addict, it falls upon me to police my own feelings and examine them when they occur so I don't succumb to mood polarities or fall prey to my own emotions. Today, like the race car driver, I can shift the metaphorical gears of my feelings with split-second precision, and if you catch me yelling at someone, you can rest assured I'm doing so on purpose and am still in control of my faculties.

And yes, I still yell sometimes. I'm not a robot. The difference is that when I yell at my son's basketball coach, I'm not shouting insults and profanities at him; I'm merely asking him (across the court) to take my opinion on how to coach as if it were gospel so our team can win the game and go home with a trophy.

Deep Dive

SELF-SOOTHING SKILLS

Cognitive reappraisal is a vital part of psychotherapy and can be found in cognitive behavioral therapy, among others. It involves shifting your perspective and looking at a problem or situation from a different angle. When coupled with mindfulness and self-compassion, it can be a formidable tool.

For this next part, let's try to reparent ourselves in the moment. Choose someone you respect or admire. It could be your best friend, your priest, or even a fictional character on your favorite television show. This person, for the purposes of this exercise, will be your avatar. Pore over past events in which there was conflict or you perhaps reacted out of fear, then look at the same situation and consider how your respected avatar would have handled it.

I've added a few examples to start you off.

SITUATION	EMOTION	MY REACTION	MY AVATAR'S REACTION
I screwed up an order at work.	I am afraid my boss doesn't like me and I will be fired.	Since I'm getting fired anyway, I may as well find another job and quit.	Own my mistake and let my boss know that I will do better moving forward.
I am gay and attracted to my straight friend.	Loneliness, anguish, longing, despair, fear.	Collect images of my friend and hoard them; contrive reasons to spend time with them alone; hug and appropriately touch them more often.	Seek some distance while I examine my feelings (are they rooted in fantasy?). Go out on more same-sex dates; become active in my community.

SITUATION	EMOTION	MY REACTION	MY AVATAR'S REACTION

EXPANDING YOUR AWARENESS

We have been focusing on our internal dynamics in order to organize our emotions and get our power back. So, too, should we turn our attention to our surroundings and align ourselves with whatever is going on around us. In this way, we can get comfortable in our own skin. For me, the best way to accomplish this is through simple meditation.

Once a day, I take a few minutes (sometimes five, sometimes 15) to simply be still and focus on my breathing. It is natural and normal, but you'd be surprised how shallow your breathing becomes during the day as stressors present and pile up on themselves. You become tense, it collects in your muscles, and you forget to just relax.

Here's what I do:

Once I've managed to relax my body by working my way up from my toes to my legs and buttocks to my torso and shoulders and then, finally, my neck and head, I am then able to send my mind out into the world.

I focus on the sounds around me. First, I focus on the quiet ticking of the clock beside my desk, and then the quiet hum of the fan inside my computer and the soft drone of the mini fridge in my office. With these sounds quietly guiding me, I expand my mind even further, taking in the sounds of traffic outside my window and the staccato sounds of birds chirping and children playing.

I allow myself to simply *be*. I don't think about myself or my problems. I don't think about other people, places, or things. This is my time to commune with my surroundings, and I use it to emotionally reset my harried feelings and just calm down. I focus on my breathing, oxygenating my blood with deep, soothing inhales while listening to the wind rustling the trees outside or the laughter of people walking by.

I focus on things other than myself for a few minutes, and I let myself *relax*.

Your meditation practice can encompass the same ritual. Keep a meditation journal for a few days. Set your intention and then write about what it was like for you afterward: What were your results? Remember to keep it simple. Meditation is about taking a step back; it shouldn't complicate things.

Here's an example to get you started.

MY INTENTION	THE RESULT
To step away from the stress of my relationship with him/her/them	I still have love feelings for him/her/them, but I feel good about taking care of myself. I feel calm.

Deep Dive

GRIEF AND LOSS

The ending of a relationship can result in feelings of intense grief and loss. After all, the relationship has, for all intents and purposes, died. The love addict experiences this loss with no real learning attached—there were no tangible memories made, no outcomes, no lessons learned. We suffer the anguish and pain of rejection without ever really processing it, and we almost always repeat the patterns with new partners without ever realizing that the patterns we've laid down have, over time, become the maze we find ourselves trapped in.

This next writing assignment is about taking a look at how we respond to grief and process loss. Write quickly, without thinking too hard on the answers. No one else is ever going to read this but you. Again, I am asking you to be as honest as possible to provide an idea of where you're at with unresolved grief or pain.

If the response proves to be emotionally taxing, take a break and come back to the exercise when you feel stronger and more yourself. Unpacking grief and loss can be difficult because it means taking long looks at bad memories. Be kind to yourself and be sure to practice self-care when completing the exercise. Don't beat yourself up for any shortcomings—no one gets it right the first time! There may not be enough space on these pages to complete the exercise; you can continue in your own journal or do the whole exercise in your own journal so you won't feel limited by the space on the page.

1. In looking back over past relationships, which one(s) did you lie to other people about? List the person's name and talk about how you lied about your partner's behavior in an effort to appear like the perfect couple.

....

....

....

....

....

2. In looking back over your life, think about relationships that have come to an end. List each person's name and talk about the days (or weeks) after the breakup. How did you feel when the relationship ended? It is important to use as much of your emotional vocabulary here as possible—*use your words*. Be sure to mention who broke up with whom. If it was you who ended the relationship, how did it make you feel? If it was the other person, did you see it coming? Did it end after a lot of trying, or did the relationship merely run its course and abruptly come to an end?

....

....

....

....

....

....

....

....

....

....

....

....

....

....

....

....

....

3. In looking back over your life, which relationship was the most painful to lose and why? (This could be the death of a beloved pet or the end of a marriage, a fight with a friend that was never resolved or even an affair that ended.) Grief and loss present themselves in our lives in a number of ways. Dig deep. What happened? How did you deal with it? We will circle back to this later, but for now let's just try to get as much of it written down as we can. You are strong and you can do this, and I am right here with you every step of the way.

....

....

....

....

....

....

....

....

....

....

....

....

....

....

....

....

....

MANAGE YOUR EMOTIONS

There is a common misconception that feelings are bad. No one says this out loud, but our culture dictates that, sure, you can have your feelings—*just don't have them in public*. Growing up, children are often told to "stop crying" or to "be quiet." This teaches us to hide our feelings while also subtly teaching us that feelings are bad. This is reinforced in preschool and kindergarten when socialization begins, and we learn to be polite and say "please" and "thank you" and learn not to hit other people when we are angry or are allowed to run and hide when we are sad. Many dramatic changes have occurred in our school systems over the years, and children today are taught to manage their feelings better, but the core system remains in place because, in order for us to function as a society, we all need to learn *how to be polite* at a very young age.

Many of my clients have great difficulty managing their emotions. They scream and cry when a favorite blouse is ruined in the wash and, consequently, take it out on their partner; or they rage in traffic and find themselves in fistfights at intersections. None of them are bad people; they merely have great difficulty managing their emotions. More often than not, we discover *why* they have such difficulty and then take steps to help them gain better control over their emotions, but sometimes the process can be challenging, with lots of stops and starts. Having intense emotions is never a bad thing as long as those emotions are regulated and expressed in appropriate ways.

It's not all about overt reactions, though. Research tells us that as much as 80 percent of our emotional communication is nonverbal. We rely on body language and facial expressions to tell us what others are feeling, but we are sometimes oblivious to what we are communicating to others. When I was angry, my girlfriend would ask me if I was all right, and I would answer, "I'm fine," and then slam a cupboard shut as I was reaching for a glass. I'm not proud of the passive-aggressive communication (I found it childish even at the time), but that was the best I could do at the time. Forgiving myself for past behaviors played a huge part in my emotional development as an adult, but changing those behaviors took time.

As we've discussed so far, many feelings are more than they seem, and some feelings can be overwhelming. In the beginning, I found an axiom that helped me manage and regulate my emotional outbursts because of its sheer simplicity. It boiled down to these three simple points:

1. Does it need to be said?

2. Does it need to be said right now?

3. Does it need to be said by me?

I cannot begin to tell you how much drama I avoided by asking those simple questions. Providing a stopgap to venting feelings is a game changer. Using our emotions is often 100 times better than being governed by them. When we learn to manage our emotions, we develop the ability to make decisions that yield wonderful consequences instead of drastic ones. Asking questions after introspection is a helpful means to that end. After all, unless you're in a hazmat suit in a bank full of hostages wondering, *Do I cut the blue wire or the green wire?*, very few things you encounter need to be resolved in that exact moment. When strong feelings arise around situations, you are allowed to say things like, "Let me think about it and get back to you," or "Give me a minute," and use the time to check in with yourself and ask:

1. How do I feel about this?

2. How do I *really* feel about this? (Remember the Feeling Wheel?)

3. What outcome do I want?

4. How will my reaction affect others?

5. Will my own emotional needs be met?

6. How can I express myself in this situation appropriately?

7. Do I need more time?

The more you do it, the more reflexive it will become. Today, I rarely need to distance myself from a situation to gauge how I feel about it. I know my feelings and manage them better than I ever did before. What's more, I know how to take care of myself emotionally, which makes me feel better about myself emotionally. And you will, too.

DEAR JOHN

A "Dear John" letter is written to a romantic partner to inform them that the relationship is over. The term was popularized during World War II, when women would write letters to their soldiers explaining that they could not wait for them to return home and had found someone else to love.

In this exercise, let's write a letter to someone who was wrong for us and tell them that we've moved on. Use your newfound emotional vocabulary to express how this person really made you feel and why you need to end things. It doesn't matter if this person rejected you or broke up with you. It doesn't matter if this is a person you are currently involved with. Nor does it matter if this person is someone who doesn't even know you're alive.

What matters is that you are addressing someone who is or was wrong for you and that you tell them the truth about how you feel. You do not need to be altruistic in this endeavor or worry about what they will say or how they'll react. This letter is just between us, and it will give us an opportunity to explore the truth using everything you've learned about yourself so far.

Say what you need to say, and use words that shine a light on what you really feel. Take your time.

And take your power back.

Dear _____,

....

....

....

....

....

....

....

....

....

FLIP THROUGH YOUR EMOTIONAL ROLODEX

I'm not exactly sure whether the word *Rolodex* has any relevance or meaning to the digerati, but in the old days, contact information was stored on a device by this name that sat on your desk. It was a rolling series of index cards that professionals used to keep and maintain client information, all of which was readily available at their fingertips at all times. But picture this: What if, instead of contact information, your Rolodex contained information about romantic experiences? And it corresponded with their emotional content?

For this next exercise, let's look at any intense love affair you may have had (it can even be an unrequited love) and list your feelings around each experience. We will come back to it later. Be as honest as possible. I've listed a couple of examples to get you started.

EXPERIENCE	EMOTION
Walking in Central Park with Rachel.	I felt loved, adored, complete, happy, fulfilled, young, eager, proud, satisfied, inspired.
Rachel in the hospital (skiing accident; broken leg).	I felt afraid in the ambulance, inadequate. I blamed myself and was angry and worried. In the hospital I felt lost, confused, scared, and worried. I was selfish and hated myself for worrying about what this would mean for our sex life. I felt fatherly and wanted to protect her and care for her. I felt pity and compassion for her because she was in pain.

EXPERIENCE	EMOTION

CELEBRATE SMALL VICTORIES

For a week, write about what action you've taken to successfully manage your feelings. Did you extract yourself from an argument before something hurtful was said? Write about it. Tell me everything that happened. Did you draw a boundary and ask for a few moments to make a decision? Did you want to commit an act of self-destruction, no matter how small, but thought better of it? I want to hear about it here. For the love addict, impulse control is key. Bookmark this page and come back to it throughout the week. Let's see what kind of strides you can make in a week's time in learning how to manage feelings and self-regulate emotions. Don't list the setbacks, only the success stories. You can do this!

....

....

....

....

....

....

....

....

....

....

....

....

....

....

....

KEY TAKEAWAYS AND REFLECTIONS

We cannot consciously control what and when we feel. But hopefully we've begun to develop an understanding of why we feel certain emotions when triggered as well as how we typically react to any given situation. We no longer live in caves, so the fight-or-flight mechanism in our brains, although still very active, isn't always reliable. We don't need our body's fight-or-flight mechanism to get through heavy traffic, for example, yet sometimes it's triggered this way. There are things we are afraid of that we shouldn't be afraid of, and information is power.

As we create a more sophisticated emotional vocabulary, we also develop the courage and ability to speak our truths and move past an irrational fear of asking for what we want in relationships and life. We stop being influenced by emotional triggers as we gain the ability to acknowledge them and make better choices for ourselves.

When we learn how to finally trust our intuition and listen to our feelings, our individual paths become easier to walk. Taking time out of our day-to-day lives to check in with ourselves and ask ourselves how we are really feeling is a means to that end.

CHAPTER FIVE

Change Your Relationships

Many people are unaware of the power they have to transform their lives. They wander the earth like the Disney character Dumbo—not dumb, mind you, just oblivious to the fact that he didn't need a magic feather his friend had given him; he could fly on his own. In this respect, the love addict is a lot like Dumbo. Granted, they often need a little motivational push, but once activated, a love addict living in recovery is a formidable force of nature. Courageous act after courageous act, the love addict seizes their power back and begins to make decisions that yield joyful, transformative consequences instead of terribly painful ones.

Thus far in this workbook, we've heroically tackled a lot of inside stuff. But what happens when that same analytic eye is used to survey our surroundings? *And what if that analytic eye is powered by insight?*

UNDERSTANDING LOVE ADDICTION'S EFFECT ON ROMANTIC RELATIONSHIPS

For the love addict, DAY ONE is the best day of their life. They wake up beside the object of their affection, and the pleasure centers of their brains are lit up like the night sky on the Fourth of July. The possibilities are endless, transporting them to fantasies of long walks on the beach, engaging conversations at patio cafés, slow dancing in nightclubs—you name it, they've imagined it. Everything is perfect and wonderful. Because they're still in Day One.

For the love addict, the endless, obsessive search for the perfect romantic relationship always supersedes commitment to their own happiness and well-being. Like the drug addict, the love addict is always searching for the next big high, and like the alcoholic, they usually pursue this regardless of consequence. A love addict will pine away for an unavailable individual and ignore true prospective partners because of a fear of intimacy. Or, desperate for the validation of being the source of someone else's happiness, the love addict will set aside their own wants and needs and sacrifice their voice in the relationship, inviting misery and a self-imposed solitude into their lives. On Day One, the love addict is happier than ever. But by Day One Hundred, the love addict is either still desperate and alone or desperate and alone while trapped in a relationship. Worse, we discover that the love addict wasn't pursuing love at all! No matter how many variances we apply, it all boils down to the only thing any love addict is truly concerned with: *limerence*.

Coined by psychologist Dorothy Tennov in her book *Love and Limerence*, the term *limerence* is defined by her as "an unhealthy obsessive state in which an individual becomes all-consumed with securing or maintaining emotional reciprocation from their object of affection, known as the limerent object." Limerence is best described by its attributes rather than its seemingly negative connotations:

→ Constant obsessive thoughts about the limerent object
→ A desperate need for reciprocation of love feelings
→ Acute dependency of mood on the limerent object's actions, directly tied into a very sophisticated reward system where highs and lows are determined by attention received from the limerent object

→ Inability to acknowledge or develop intimate feelings for more appropriate or available individuals

→ Fulfilling emotional needs despite unrequited feelings by living in the fantasy of what might be or what once was

→ Altering plans or setting aside one's own wants and needs to ensure the limerent object's wants, desires, and needs are met

In limerence, potential problems (what I call *red flags*) are easily overlooked due to the excitement and intensity of finally finding The One. This is typical for any relationship, sure, but the love addict chooses to *live* in limerence, using it as an escape from stress or pressure in much the same way an addict uses heroin.

The object of their affection becomes the drug, and without it they simply fall apart. Even worse, the love addict—having reveled in countless Day Ones—has a poor concept of the natural evolution of relationships and almost no concept of true partnership. They tend to idolize their partners, placing them high on a pedestal while desperately vying for both attention and approval. They will sacrifice friendships, time, money, and resources all to assuage the fear of losing this person or for the hope for gaining their favor. But does this make the love addict happy?

The easy answer is yes. These relationships fulfill the love addict in unique and complicated ways. It's all they've ever known—the patterns for these relationships were laid down so early in their development, the only proof the love addict has that it is at all bad is the anguish they feel when they get what they are looking for—a toxic relationship.

Breaking the cycle of their addiction is never attractive to the love addict, because breaking the cycle means changing how their relationships work. And that means focusing on themselves instead of their limerent objects.

Think about it: The love addict is a person whose ability to self-regulate is directly tied to the feelings associated with Day One romance—feelings that are dependent on the love addict's own ability to make someone else happy. They are not addicted to love; they are addicted to limerence. And all of this hinges on the addict's penchant for denial. The love addict will usually blame their limerent object for their own consequences and unhappiness. This is because, subconsciously, the love addict doesn't want to give up their drug. *They want to feel the neurochemical rush of new love.*

Again, let's look at the typical heroin addict. Recovery for them means never using heroin ever again. This is a healthy decision because heroin will kill them. The treatment for substance use disorder is abstinence.

Love addiction, however, has to be treated like an eating disorder. You cannot remove food from the equation or the person with the eating disorder will starve and die. Long-term abstinence is not realistic.

The love addict heals by learning how to develop and maintain healthy, noncompulsive, reciprocal relationships. These relationships are not as neurochemically intense, but they are substantial, robust, and fulfilling, and offer the love addict true intimacy and connection.

ARE YOU IN A CODEPENDENT RELATIONSHIP?

Admittedly, love is a two-way street. People often enjoy taking care of one another. But in a codependent relationship, your identity, happiness, and disposition are defined by the other person. You have a passive voice in the relationship, and your partner has a dominant one. Sometimes that person will gain satisfaction (whether consciously or subconsciously) from having control over you and making decisions about how you will live. And they will have that power because you will have given it to them.

Answer these next 20 questions, and let's see how you fare in regard to codependence. As always, take a moment to examine each statement before deciding whether it is true for you or not.

1. It is hard for me to communicate in a relationship.

   ☐ TRUE
   ☐ FALSE

2. I have difficulty identifying my feelings.

   ☐ TRUE
   ☐ FALSE

3. It is challenging for me to make decisions in a relationship.

   ☐ TRUE
   ☐ FALSE

4. I worry about abandonment and/or rejection.

   ☐ TRUE
   ☐ FALSE

5. I have an obsessive need for attention and approval.

   ☐ TRUE
   ☐ FALSE

6. I value the approval of others more than I value myself.

   ☐ TRUE
   ☐ FALSE

7. I often take responsibility for the actions of others; I am the hero in my relationships.

   ☐ TRUE
   ☐ FALSE

8. My relationships have affected my reputation.

   ☐ TRUE
   ☐ FALSE

9. I have remained in relationships where I was unhappy for longer than I should have.

   ☐ TRUE
   ☐ FALSE

10. I spend a great amount of time thinking about other people and relationships in my life.

   ☐ TRUE
   ☐ FALSE

11. I sometimes manipulate others to get what I want or reach my goals.

   ☐ TRUE
   ☐ FALSE

12. When I am in an argument, I will lose because I would rather be wrong than lose the other person.

   ☐ TRUE
   ☐ FALSE

13. It's hard for me to say no when someone asks for help.

   ☐ TRUE
   ☐ FALSE

14. I remain loyal, even when someone is harmful to me.

☐ TRUE
☐ FALSE

15. After a fight or disagreement, I often feel the need to get even.

☐ TRUE
☐ FALSE

16. I am a scorekeeper; I drag old hurts into current conversations.

☐ TRUE
☐ FALSE

17. I have borrowed money to finance my loved one's addiction.

☐ TRUE
☐ FALSE

18. I have difficulty defining and maintaining boundaries out of fear of losing people.

☐ TRUE
☐ FALSE

19. I need to help, and feel rejected when another person doesn't want my help or is clearly not taking my advice.

☐ TRUE
☐ FALSE

20. My shame and low self-esteem create anxiety and fear about being judged, rejected, or abandoned.

☐ TRUE
☐ FALSE

If you answered TRUE to 10 or more of these questions, you may be codependent.

Deep Dive

TAKE STOCK

Many would argue that the two main ingredients to successful pair bonding in a relationship are timing and chemistry, but for the love addict, we must also factor in compatibility. How much of yourself and your values have you set aside or suppressed in order to be in a relationship? *How compatible are you in reality?*

The following questions are designed to provide a bird's-eye view of either the relationship you are in or any past relationships you may have had. Be brave, take your time, and answer each question as truthfully as you can.

1. If asked, which of you would say they wear the pants in the relationship?

   a. Me.

   b. My partner.

   c. We are equal.

2. As a couple, do you regularly laugh together?

   a. No. We don't have the same sense of humor.

   b. Yes. I laugh mostly when they do; I rarely laugh at what I myself find funny when we are together.

   c. Yes. We laugh together sometimes and enjoy the same comedy shows.

   d. We share a laugh most days and it makes us feel connected.

3. How connected are you when it comes to sex?

   a. Sex for us is mechanical.

   b. We were made for each other. There are no complaints in this area of our relationship.

   c. I find myself having to perform more often than not. Sex is a service I provide to keep them happy and/or ensure they never stray.

   d. We are great at cuddling but bad at sex.

4. How connected are you through religion and spirituality?

   a. We share the same spiritual beliefs.

   b. We are of two different religions and we argue about it.

   c. We are of two different religions and respect each other's choices.

   d. One of us is an atheist.

   e. We have very similar spiritual beliefs and have engaging conversations about them.

5. How do your political views match?

   a. We avoid talking about politics.

   b. We argue about our political views.

   c. On one or two talking points, we agree, but on others we usually "agree to disagree."

   d. I have adopted their political views in order to maintain harmony in the relationship.

6. If an outsider were to question our compatibility, I would say:

   a. Compatibility doesn't matter. We are meant for each other.

   b. Our relationship isn't perfect, but it isn't supposed to be.

   c. We see ourselves as connected and evolved and could happily spend the rest of our lives together.

   d. This is good for now, but I am not planning to spend the rest of my life with this person.

7. How do you spend your spare time together as a couple?

   a. We shop, clean, and do chores separately.

   b. We pursue different hobbies.

   c. We argue a lot about not spending time together.

   d. I do whatever my partner enjoys doing; I'm easygoing.

8. When my partner hugs or kisses me in mixed company:

    a. I am embarrassed; I do not enjoy being claimed or owned, and/or public displays of affection make me cringe inside.

    b. I am proud to be with this person and want everyone to know it.

    c. I usually become aroused.

    d. I allow it because it is obviously something they feel they need to do at the time.

9. My partner loves me for:

    a. My soul.

    b. My body.

    c. My mind.

    d. We never talk about why we love one another, and my partner rarely pays me compliments.

10. Compared to my ex, my partner:

    a. Is exactly the same way; I have a "type."

    b. Is more affectionate.

    c. Doesn't need me as much, so I always feel clingy.

    d. Compliments and insults me but becomes angered by criticism.

Look over your responses. Do you see any patterns you wish were different or that may not be serving you in the best way? Do you see any red flags you're tempted to paint green?

Deep Dive

EMOTIONAL SELF-SOOTHING AND VALIDATION

No one is alone. Chances are, you have family or friends who love you and want what's best for you. Having said that, I feel like it's time to take another step closer to letting someone in.

This next exercise is a simple one. The thinking here is that maybe you are your own worst critic. Many of us tend to judge ourselves harshly and magnify our mistakes, but we seldom shine a bright light on our successes. The things about ourselves that we share with the people closest to us are the things we will someday share with our lovers, but we must first reacquaint ourselves with our *better* selves.

Have you ever served a plate of food to a guest and heard them say, "This is amazing! You're a terrific chef!" and you reply with, "It's not that great. I overcooked it a little."

Why do we do that? It can be argued that we are simply telling the truth, but in that instance, we are also invalidating a compliment. We're supposed to say "thank you" when someone compliments us, not invest energy into telling them they're wrong.

I'd like you to complete the following sentences. The lesson here is that if you are focusing on the negative aspects of who you are, then you are focusing on the wrong thing. Try to have fun with it–stretch yourself a little. Look back over your entire life and really focus on the things you heard that made you feel good about yourself, and write them down here.

All you have to do is finish the sentences and tell the story.

1. My friends always tell me that I'm great because I . . .

....

....

....

....

....

....

2. My best achievement in life so far was when I . . .

....

....

....

....

....

....

3. No one knows this about me, but I'm really good at . . .

....

....

....

....

....

....

4. When I'm alone and no one is watching, I really enjoy . . .

....

....

....

....

....

....

5. My parents used to say these amazing things about me, and it felt really good to hear them:

....

....

....

....

....

....

6. The thing I'm most excited about pursuing in the future is . . .

....

....

....

....

....

....

THE LAUNDRY LIST

Until they are recovering, the idea of an ideal relationship for the love addict is not a practical one. The healthier we get in recovery from love addiction, the less grief we will put up with for the sake of remaining true to ourselves and our own happiness. But great relationships are not impossible for us.

Let's start by itemizing what we want out of a real relationship. Stay away from vague ideas like "I want it to be exciting" because we don't really know that we want excitement. Heck, for some of us excitement equals conflict, and we are trying to move away from that aspect of our lives!

Take your time to imagine how your relationship should be, what the other person will be like, how they will treat you, and what they will be bringing to the table. Be as well-rounded as possible. Identify your values (see Take Stock, page 105). Include facets of your sex life. Do you want children? Do you want to travel? Will your partner have a great body? Skinny, fit, or fat—just write down what you want. If you are currently in a marriage or relationship, make a list of things you'd like to see change in order for you to be happy, so we can later compare what you want with what you have.

We'll come back to this, but for now, let's put all of our energy and focus into the list.

....

....

....

....

....

....

....

....

....

MELISSA'S DILEMMA

Melissa is an attractive 24-year-old medical student with psoriasis, a recurring skin condition that has been a source of shame for most of her adult life. Still, she is a natural beauty who dates in between flare-ups. She met Brad, another medical student, during her second year of med school, and the two hit it off. Brad is a handsome narcissist who is committed to becoming a successful surgeon. During a psoriasis flare-up, Brad was kind and sympathetic to Melissa's plight and offered on many occasions to pay for her to see a dermatologist. Melissa declined, however, and elected to stay with her own doctor. As time passed, Brad took to making fun of Melissa's skin condition in mixed company. This hurt Melissa's feelings, but she said nothing for fear that Brad would interpret her as being defensive and punish her by withholding affection. Eventually, Brad became crueler, commenting on Melissa's weight and, after lovemaking, the size of Melissa's breasts. Her studies began to suffer, and she did not do well on the most important examination of her medical education. Still, Melissa continued to see Brad. One of her friends, a psychology major, encouraged Melissa to set boundaries in the relationship and be honest with Brad about how much his words hurt her, but Melissa reiterated that she was in love with him and did not want to lose him. "Sticks and stones" became her motto, and she strapped herself in for the long haul. It was another year before Brad hit Melissa during an argument, and on her 26th birthday, he slept with another woman. Their relationship was on-again, off-again until Melissa agreed to marry Brad shortly after turning 28. After the birth of their second child, Brad divorced Melissa, leaving her for a younger woman.

By the time Melissa walked into my office, she was a remarkable but broken woman with psoriasis-ridden forearms and bleak, dark eyes. Our first session was engaging and fun, and I knew right away that there was still plenty of life in her. She loved her children and was embarking on a date later that week with a coworker who'd asked her out with verve. But we realized Melissa was codependent and needed to increase her emotional vocabulary as well as learn how to set boundaries at the beginning of the relationship. Before all that, Melissa had to learn that she was worth adoration and that she deserved to have a voice in her relationships. I am still working with her on the latter. It has been almost a year and a half, and she has made great strides. I am very proud of her, and, more importantly, *Melissa is proud of herself*.

SETTING BOUNDARIES

Boundaries are challenging for the love addict. They think that whenever they set and enforce boundaries, they run the risk of ending a relationship. An inherent people pleaser, the love addict lives in a world where the needs of others are prioritized over their own, creating unnecessary stress and anxiety because while those around them feel cared for and supported, the love addict's own needs, wants, and desires almost always go unmet. This creates resentment, which, if left unchecked, can result in insomnia, anxiety, panic attacks, and ulcers. All because they couldn't say no.

Boundaries are an important part of any relationship, platonic or romantic. It's your way of saying, "This is me, and if you cross this line, you make me feel as if you don't respect me, my feelings, or my values." Boundaries can be emotional, physical, or even proprietary. Some examples of boundaries are:

→ I need quiet time to myself in the morning so I can meditate and plan my day.

→ I am okay with texting, but I cannot text as frequently as you like.

→ I am okay with following each other on social media, but I am not okay with sharing passwords.

→ My emails are personal, and I'd rather you not use my laptop to read them.

→ I am not ready to have sex yet.

→ I don't enjoy company functions; you'll have to attend the company holiday party alone.

→ I don't like to share my food.

→ I am comfortable with and enjoy kissing and affection, but I cannot always cuddle with you when we watch television.

In relationships, *unhealthy* boundaries are usually about control. You may say to your partner, "I am going to have a party night alone with my friends, but I'll hang out with you on Saturday night" and feel as though everything is wonderful. You've communicated your need for autonomy on Friday night, and you've done so in a nonthreatening way. But if they reply with, "I don't like it when you hang out with friends; I get jealous and I know you might cheat on me," it's a sign that your partner is trying to exert control over your life as the result of trust issues that have nothing to do with you. Obeying this new, unhealthy boundary set by your partner might mean ceding control over your personal life to them, and this is usually done because we are afraid of losing the other person or hurting their feelings. Our own need to socialize with people we like is given a lower priority, and in an attempt to keep our partner happy, we even give up our need for privacy.

In unhealthy relationships, boundaries often get skewed. Unhealthy boundaries will typically look like this:

→ Always focusing on your partner's wants and needs while placing your own on the back burner
→ Playing mind games and being manipulative as opposed to communicating in a way that is open and real
→ Being unable to ask for what you want for fear of losing the other person
→ Being unable to say no to your partner without consequence or criticism
→ Checking your phone, email, or social media accounts without your permission
→ Putting you down in front of mixed company
→ Any form of physical harm
→ Possessiveness or controlling behavior

When you participate in codependent behavior and fail to establish boundaries, your partner may sometimes unwillingly or subconsciously step into the role of power and control that you yourself have set up. That is why it's important to establish boundaries at the beginning of the relationship or, at the very least, introduce them gradually so that your partner learns to understand and appreciate your needs.

In other words, be honest when possible; if not, then be honest as soon as possible.

Deep Dive
UNCHARTED TERRITORY

In looking back over your life, where have you failed to set boundaries in different relationships (not just romantic)? Use the following table as an outline for itemizing instances when your failure to speak up set up prerequisites in the relationship that made you uncomfortable or unhappy. Be as honest as possible. I've listed a couple of examples. Setting boundaries often means standing up for yourself, and I recognize that isn't always an easy thing to do. This doesn't make you any less of a person; this exercise is a helpful way to show how our lack of boundaries placed us in situations that made us unhappy.

PERSON	ACTION	UNEXPRESSED BOUNDARY
Meagan	I caught her reading my text messages over my shoulder	I never told her I felt as if my right to privacy was being invaded
My brother Tom	Bad-mouthed my girlfriend when she wasn't in the room	I never told him it angered me to hear him say hurtful things about the woman I loved

PERSON	ACTION	UNEXPRESSED BOUNDARY

Deep Dive
IN A PERFECT WORLD

Following are five situations in which boundaries need to be set. Try to think about the healthy response for each situation and write it down. I know these may be difficult situations, and your mind may tell you, "I'd never respond that way in real life"–that's okay. For now, just try to imagine the best-case scenario to get an idea of what healthy responses look like. A huge part of developing new neural pathways is in the preparation for the event; it's as important as the execution. Find a way to imagine the best version of yourself and remember: You are only as strong as you will LET yourself be.

CONFLICT: You've spent money on supplies for your home office, and you've noticed your roommate has been using your resources without your permission. You're living check to check, and the two of you have never discussed sharing items you've purchased.

RESPONSE: "I need to keep our supplies separate. If there's something of mine that you need, please ask for it."

CONFLICT: You're visiting your parents and your mother is pushing you to have seconds, despite the fact that you've already devoured a lion's share of the dinner she's prepared.

RESPONSE: "I love you for wanting to feed me, but I try not to eat when I'm not hungry. Maybe we can pack some leftovers to go?"

CONFLICT: You've had an argument with your partner. A coworker overhears you telling a friend about it over the phone and asks about it. You feel this information is personal and do not want to share it.

RESPONSE: ....

....

....

....

CONFLICT: A friendly stranger knocks at your door and wants to talk to you about their religious beliefs. You are currently in the middle of your favorite show and not interested in an exchange of ideas.

RESPONSE:..

....

....

....

CONFLICT: Your partner wants to come over for a quick rendezvous, but you know it will probably last for hours, and you need to wake up early for work. You have a long day ahead of you, and you could use the sleep.

RESPONSE:..

....

....

....

CONFLICT: Your partner wants to take you to see a horror film. The blood and gore and scares repulse and terrify you. You do not want to see this movie. Your partner has heard rave reviews and is pressuring you to see it with them.

RESPONSE:..

....

....

....

CONFLICT: A friend wants to eat at a popular restaurant. The last time you ate there, you got food poisoning, and you don't want to risk it again.

RESPONSE:..

....

....

....

CHANGING HOW YOU COMMUNICATE

We've talked about emotional vocabulary and setting boundaries, but how do these things look in real time and in real life for you? Finding one's center and speaking the truth are daunting notions for the love addict because at their core, the love addict lives in fear of never getting what they want or losing what they have. This fear paralyzes their emotional growth; they are too frightened to take the baby steps toward healing the intimate traumas that trigger their desperate need for attention and approval from their partners. I implore you: Be brave.

There are inalienable rights that we have as active participants in any relationship, be it familial, platonic, or romantic. We *have* to activate our own roles in the situations and circumstances we find ourselves in because, more often than not, any conflict that arises is of our own doing. Setting boundaries and communicating our needs are both means of waylaying that. Among these inalienable rights are:

→ **The right to say no.** You never need to justify not wanting to do something with an explanation. Communicating your feelings is important, yes, but not if it invites argument or debate. "No" is a complete answer. If you don't want to do something, that is *always* okay.

→ **The right to change your mind.** Our emotions change from day to day, sometimes minute to minute. It is never okay for someone to make you feel guilty for changing your mind about anything. You have the right. Stand your ground.

→ **The right to ask for what you want.** In every relationship, it is important to have a voice of your own. Being an adult means doing what you need to do to ensure that your needs are met. Unfortunately, being an adult also means sometimes having to accept that you might not always get what you want, but you always have the right to ask.

→ **The right to expect honesty.** Lying is a cooperative process. When someone lies to you, in order for it to become valid, you need to accept the lie. Don't. You have the right to ask questions if you are feeling duped, and you have the right to expect honesty. No one is allowed to be angry with you for acting on the information they gave you. If you sense a problem, and your partner says they are fine and you move forward in response, they cannot be angry with you for neglecting their needs. You aren't a mind reader.

→ **The right to make mistakes.** Everyone does. Not everyone suffers from low self-esteem; some of us merely hold ourselves to an impossibly high standard. It's okay to make mistakes. It's okay to even fail some of the time; it's how we get experience. If someone berates you or makes you feel "less than" because you made a mistake, try to set a boundary by not standing for it. None of us are perfect. We are all mostly just rolling with the punches. Don't let others beat you up for your mistakes, and for the love of God, try not to beat yourself up for them either.

→ **The right not to be responsible for others' feelings, behavior, or problems.** You are your own person, and while it is okay to empathize with others, you should not silence your voice nor place your needs at a low priority in order to spare someone else's feelings. We've explored diplomatic ways to communicate your needs and establish boundaries. Be creative but firm. This is a tenet of basic self-care.

Deep Dive
SAY WHAT YOU MEAN TO SAY

Let's practice communicating our feelings. We're going to come up with 20 ways to say no. I'll start you off with five. It's okay if you can't come up with 15 more, but please take your time with this exercise and really try—for you.

Afterward, practice saying these aloud. Do it while you're doing something productive, like cooking your dinner or folding your laundry.

1. This doesn't work for me.

2. I can't do that for you.

3. I've decided not to.

4. I'm not comfortable with this.

5. I don't want to do that.

6. ....

....

7. ....

....

8. ....

....

9. ....

....

10. ....

....

11. ....

....

12. ....

....

13. ....

....

14. ....

....

15. ....

....

16. ....

....

17. ....

....

18. ....

....

19. ....

....

20. ....

....

Deep Dive

FIND YOUR CORE VALUES

It's hard to stand by your convictions when you don't know what they are! With this exercise, let's try to identify some of your core beliefs. You can have as many as you like, but for now, let's choose seven. Look over this list, then check off the boxes that you feel represent seven of your core values. I've even left a few spaces for you to write in your own core values if they should occur to you during this exercise.

☐ Dependability   ☐ Passion

☐ Open-Mindedness   ☐ Loyalty

☐ Honesty   ☐ Integrity

☐ Consistency   ☐ Respect

☐ Good Humor   ☐ Sportsmanship

☐ Compassion   ☐ Faith

☐ Optimism   ☐ Honor

☐ Courage   ☐ Justice

☐ Patriotism   ☐ Family

☐ Environmentalism

☐ ....

☐ ....

☐ ....

☐ ....

☐ ....

☐ ....

☐ ....

☐ ....

COMMITMENT TO CHANGE

List the seven core values you've chosen, and then write about how you've implemented them in your day-to-day life this week. And remember: Convictions mean something only if you stand by them when it's *inconvenient*. Not every core value will come up every day, but this exercise is about how you react when they do. Write the date down and then write about which core value came up for you and how you reinforced it in your life.

1. ....

....

....

....

....

2. ....

....

....

....

....

3. ....

....

....

....

....

4. ....

....

....

....

....

5. ....

....

....

....

....

6. ....

....

....

....

....

7. ....

....

....

....

....

Did you notice something in this exercise? *In order to reinforce a core value, you almost always need to draw a boundary.*

KEY TAKEAWAYS AND REFLECTIONS

As we delve further and further into why the love-addicted person behaves the way they do, we discover basic, fundamental truths about ourselves. Even if we don't like everything we learn, this knowledge allows us to focus on making dramatic changes in our lives so we can be happy. The things we've uncovered thus far may ring as true for you as they do for me. If that is the case, I'd like you to go back to the very first exercise I gave you (page 5) and study it. Try to identify why you developed these patterns of behavior. Look for the root causes of these five tendencies for you:

1. You are afraid of not getting what you want or losing what you have.

2. You put others' needs and feelings first.

3. You believe that setting boundaries will threaten your relationship or drive people away.

4. You are afraid of negative reactions from others.

5. You are afraid to ask for what you want.

When reading your very first exercise, stop and meditate on how much the formative experiences in your life have shaped you into who you are today. Now remember that you can change at any time. Someone once said, *"If your parents left you out in the rain when you were nine years old, shame on them; if you're still standing out in the rain when you're 20, shame on you."* Granted, I don't think shaming people into change is ever a good idea, because it creates more trauma. To me, this statement is more about pointing out that as adults, we have the power to enact real change in ourselves and our lives so that we can move toward being genuinely happy.

All we have to do is do the work. And you're here.

CHAPTER SIX

Practice Self-Care

Every time we fly, we hear as part of the safety talk, "Place the oxygen mask on yourself first before attempting to help or assist others." This kind of thinking is challenging for the love addict and even more so for the codependent personality because our first instinct is to make sure our lover's needs are met before our own. That first instinct is toxic.

FOCUS ON YOURSELF

Our needs are just as important as anyone else's. Somewhere along the way, we lost that message. We met someone and fell in love and became so obsessed with not losing the other person that we placed our partners' needs before our own. I'm not only referring to physical needs; I am also referring to emotional needs. Having a voice in any relationship is important for us, not only as love addicts but also as healthy human beings. We need to embrace the freedom of living and choosing for ourselves.

We've talked about mindfulness and meditation. For me, folding in a few minutes every day to simply breathe and send my mind out into the city around me is enough for one day, but in the beginning, it wasn't an easy practice to adopt. I needed to make a conscious effort to check in with myself and focus on me and me alone. This was an enormous undertaking because my knee-jerk reaction was always to rush and take care of *her* needs first (in my mind, this placed me, in her eyes, in the role of The Hero). I needed to reparent myself and learn how to take care of my own physical and emotional needs; I needed to create a space to *breathe*.

This seems like commonsense stuff—until you try enacting it into a daily practice. Basic self-care is a vital part of our treatment that should not be shirked. When we take time to check in with ourselves, this experience helps inform both our decisions and our actions. In the beginning, I used a simple notepad to document my needs, in the form of a to-do list. I had to teach myself to check things off. In many instances, that meant standing up for myself, which was not an easy thing for me to do at first. I had to learn how to be forgiving to myself whenever I was unable to follow through on a task and to respect the process.

Learning basic self-care practices is daunting because we are chipping away at all of our bad habits and ideas in an attempt to expose the "real" us. It is frightening because so much of what we cling to are old "elephant ideas" that keep us shackled and immobile and unable to grow. But we are better than that. We are stronger than that. If the love addict is anything, they are tenacious and enduring. We've had to be. How else would we have survived our crippling love lives until now?

Deep Dive
CHIP AWAY AT YOUR SHACKLES

This is a simple but challenging exercise in that it dovetails with your daily mindfulness exercises. After meditating or simply remaining calm to organize your mind, make a list of things that come up for you or items you should take care of in the next 24 hours. Unlike other exercises, items on this list can be rolled over into the following day if they have not been completed or if they seem likely to rear their ugly heads again. Bear in mind it is entirely possible that nothing could come up for you at all. This does not mean you've done anything wrong. We are learning mindfulness here, and if introspection yields nothing but serenity and peace, it is still a successful session. If something does come up, however, *be mindful of it and write it down*. I've included some examples to start you off.

Jeffrey	I need to ask him about that trainer he suggested.
Brandon	I need to talk to him about Mom's 60th birthday party. We need to settle on a restaurant.
Cherries	Cherries are in season. I love them. I cannot count on David to pick them up for me; I need to go to the market and buy them myself. I deserve to enjoy them while watching television tonight.
Susan	I need to draw a boundary with her financially. I don't earn enough money to support us both yet; she needs to pull her own weight.

Deep Dive
USE THE DIPSTICK

For an automobile engine to function properly, we must keep the oil topped off and fresh. We use a dipstick to check the level as well as the color and density of the fluid, so we know when maintenance is required. Wouldn't it be helpful if we could see our own levels as clearly? *Sometimes simply remembering to eat can be an act of self-care.* I cannot begin to tell you how many times I book my day without remembering to leave a spot open for lunch. And I love food!

Self-care for the love addict requires a daily check-in on five areas of your life. There are many schools of thought as to what constitutes a good self-care practice, but for me, I like to limit it to these five: Where am I physically, emotionally, spiritually, in relationships, and financially?

Using a scale of 1 to 5 (5 represents optimal success in that area), rate each of the following check-ins *and then review the list* to determine which areas need some attention in order for you to establish good self-care practices:

_____ I went to the gym (exercised, bicycled, went for a long walk, etc.).

_____ I had a good laugh.

_____ I did not visit my love object's workplace or social hangouts.

_____ I spent quality time with a friend.

_____ I used my increased emotional vocabulary to communicate my feelings.

_____ I spent time doing an activity with others (went to a movie, went out to dinner, etc.).

_____ I asked for help at work or delegated tasks to reduce burnout on my end.

_____ I listened to music I enjoy.

_____ I meditated.

_____ I participated in my religious or spiritual practice.

_____ I spent time alone with no outside distractions (unplugged from technology).

_____ I took a nap or rested when I was tired.

_____ I did not allow myself to grow hungry (carved time out of my day
to eat).

_____ I sat down and reviewed and/or paid my bills.

_____ I spent time connecting with my pet (if applicable).

_____ I made my bed after sleeping in it.

_____ I got to know my coworkers better (socialized with them).

_____ I spent quality time with my partner.

_____ I took a relaxing bath or shower (as opposed to a hurried one).

_____ I did my laundry.

_____ I cleaned my home.

_____ I took time to do something I love (hobby, favorite television show,
gardening, etc.).

_____ I took time to massage a relationship with a friend I've fallen out of
touch with.

_____ I did my dishes.

_____ I resisted the urge to check out my love object's social media.

List items that ranked below a 3. Commit to working on these in order to
practice better self-care. Select three to focus on daily:

....

....

....

....

....

....

....

Deep Dive
PULL WEEDS

In our day-to-day lives, there are obvious obstacles that prevent us from practicing basic self-care. Identifying these obstacles is just as important as implementing self-care practices. At the root of all the eye-rolling at this simple task? *Contempt prior to investigation.* As love addicts, we are so attuned to the needs of others that we scoff at the opportunity to investigate fulfilling our own needs. This is something we do when presented with the chance to recover and heal from our addiction to other people, places, or things. It all points toward the love addict seeking emotional gratification from an outside source. Instead, let's learn how to get comfortable embracing any opportunity we have to look within.

This next exercise is pretty straightforward. Answer these questions as honestly as possible and investigate ways to change how you take care of yourself:

1. What self-care habits did you employ before you met that person but you are no longer employing?

....

....

....

....

....

2. What's standing in your way of practicing each self-care habit you used to love?

....

....

....

....

....

3. What's the best way for you to return to taking better care of yourself?

....

....

....

....

....

4. Imagine what it would be like to implement one self-care practice in your life. It can be something that you have either abandoned or would like to try for the first time. What self-care practice would it be? (Yoga? The gym? Meditation? Live music? Swimming? The sky's the limit.) How would you introduce that self-care practice into your life today?

....

....

....

....

....

5. What positive affirmations help remind you of your value? When listing the affirmations, be sure to do them in the first person (use the word "I") and associate a feeling with it (such as, "*It makes me happy that I am an honest person*" or "*I pride myself on my dependability*").

....

....

....

....

....

JESSICA'S DILEMMA

Jessica is a case study in codependence and anxious attachment. Her boyfriend uses drugs and is out of state at the moment. She fears he will have sex with other women while away. Jessica is a very attractive, extremely bright 37-year-old professional woman and feels that since she's already invested two years into this guy, it's too late to start over and date other men. She wants to get pregnant and have a baby. She wants to build a family with her boyfriend, and she rejects the notion of kicking him to the curb. Her fear is that she will push him away if she reaches out and complains about his failure to return phone calls or text messages in a timely manner. She does not respond to the idea that he's wrong for her, but she *did* respond to the notion of being too needy.

The work is in emphasizing her independence and convincing her to not be as needy for him so she can feel better about herself. If she can have some distance and not become needy, maybe she will see the truth, which is that she does not need him.

What's more, if she isn't so needy, perhaps he will gravitate toward her and be more emotionally available. ***Maybe we can get him to chase her.*** Any other tack will alienate her and move her away from healing. My goal is to guide her to take action when she becomes emotionally independent. Perhaps she will leave him, perhaps she will not, but we will have enabled her to make her decisions from a position of power instead of hapless fear and need.

PRACTICE SELF-COMPASSION AND SELF-LOVE

"Comments like these have weight, and they affect us because this is how we talk to ourselves. These comments ride in on the names we call ourselves internally ... but know that, without the internal self-hate, comments like these are powerless."

—@THEJEFFREYMARSH, TIKTOK PERSONALITY, WHEN ADDRESSING BEING CALLED A "FREAK"

I once had a guesthouse that served as my home office. My clients would come by, and we would sit for the requisite hour as they processed whatever was coming up for them. One client in particular arrived a few minutes late for his appointment and sat in the oversize, comfortable sofa I'd provided. "DAMMIT!" he exclaimed and stood up abruptly. "I forgot to lock my car! I'm such an idiot!"

As he moved toward the door, I motioned for him to forget about the car and sit down for a moment, because the language was very telling. We discovered that his father would reprimand him often, calling him "idiot" in the process, and this language became my client's self-talk.

Many of us engage in this every day: unconscious, negative self-talk that informs and reinforces our narrative. We call ourselves things like "stupid" or "dumb" or "moron" on a nearly daily basis. Learning how to give an equal or greater voice to our good or better aspects isn't something we do reflexively. We need to learn how to be nice to ourselves. Psychologist Carl Jung often spoke of the mind's "shadow," an aspect of ourselves of which we are completely unaware. I believe this to be congruent with the voices of our parents (or, at least, it is programmed by our parents and often sounds like our own inner voice). This duality exists within us and can often be likened to that voice that says things in our minds like *"Damn it, I forgot to put the* milk back in the fridge!" or "I have to remember to pick the kids up from school later, since Marjorie has to work late." This inner voice is also the voice that reprimands us or says things like "She's going to leave me if I don't take care of her needs" or "He won't like me if I stop wearing that color he once said he loves so much on me" or "You idiot, you left your coffee cup on the roof of the car!"

If committing estimable acts is the precursor to building self-esteem, then practicing self-compassion and self-love is the precursor to creating a space where self-soothing and self-awareness are even possible. Before we can do that, however, we need to decide what language we are going to use to attain that goal and what actions we are going to take to get there.

First, we need to identify the harsh, critical voices or feelings we ascribe to ourselves. Whenever external stressors are coupled with internalized self-deprecation, a kind of perfect storm ensues that—whether we are aware of it or not—dramatically affects our worldview and triggers us. The thinking that some outside person, place, or thing will fix us tends to take over, and it hijacks our decision-making.

For example, college student Joe is having a bad day. His loved one is always at the library. Joe doesn't even realize this, but he has already decided to skip his afternoon class in order to spend time at the library in the hopes of connecting with his loved one, because seeing them will give him the dopamine rush he is craving. Joe's internal reward system is hardwired to his loved one. Once triggered, without conscious intervention, Joe will find himself compelled to do whatever it takes to feel good—like miss class and wander around the library looking for them. In this case, Joe is using his loved one instead of a drug as an outside remedy for an inside problem.

But what if Joe intervenes in his own behavior? What if he simply gives himself permission to have a bad day? What if Joe's internal dialogue is now, "There are good days and there are bad days, but in and of myself, nothing has changed. I am still amazing and talented and worthy of adoration. I am whole and complete just as I am. I love being me."?

By training yourself to recognize negative self-talk and meet it with what you've discovered to be true while doing the work, you are activating the highest form of self-care, self-compassion, and self-love imaginable.

Deep Dive

THE GRATITUDE LIST

Upon waking, make a list of 10 things for which you are grateful. The love addict tends to focus on thoughts that reinforce the negative narrative they have constructed. Gratitude lists subconsciously force the mind to redirect itself. Once redirected, the mind sometimes has trouble finding its way back toward "stinkin' thinkin'." We are sick people getting better, but getting better is never simply an act of will; *we need to do the work*.

The point of the exercise is to dig deep and come up with 10 different items every day for 30 days. I have included my own list as a reference. Good luck!

1. My children

2. My vision

3. The good feeling from helping others

4. The baristas at the smoothie shop

5. My dog

6. Being able to love without expecting anything in return

7. Bruce Springsteen

8. My home

9. My ability to feed myself

10. My lost luggage being found by the airline

Now you try:

1. ....

2. ....

3. ....

4. ....

5. ....

6. ....

7. ....

8. ....

9. ....

Every week or so, look over your past entries and think about whether your mindset has shifted. Consider how you may be feeling differently.

Deep Dive
WHAT I DID FOR LOVE

Not many people are aware of how remarkable or amazing they are. Love addicts are usually afflicted with various codependent traits, but most are typically what one would call good people.

For this next exercise, let's get a snapshot of who you really are as a person. Again, this is just between us and extremely private, so I am going to ask you to dig deep and be as honest as possible. Answer the questions to the best of your ability, wait a day, and then read what you wrote with fresh eyes. This is our Identified Patient. This is who we are trying to help. And this is a person worth saving. Use your own journal to make sure you have enough space, and get it all out on paper. Good luck!

1. In looking back over your life, write about an occasion where you helped someone who was suffering. Had a child fallen and skinned their knee? Did you comfort someone at a funeral? Did a close friend go through a breakup? Did your pet have a frightening experience and look to you for support? Write about any occasion where you had to show up for someone else. Tell me about it. What feelings were they having? What feelings do you remember having? What was the direct result of your "being there"?

....

....

....

....

....

....

....

....

....

....

2. Let your mind go back in time and find your childhood self during a difficult time in your life. Write a letter of encouragement to them to help them get through it. Be sure to choose an instance you've already survived. Be loving and supportive. Help them in the way that only *you* can. Choose your words carefully and remember that you are talking to a child.

....

....

....

....

....

....

....

....

....

....

....

....

....

....

....

....

....

....

....

3. Write a poem about how it feels to be held by another human being. It doesn't need to rhyme, but it needs to be thoughtful and carefully considered. Close your eyes and remember what it was like to be held by someone you felt truly loved you. Write about how that felt. Don't limit yourself to a haiku; make it a substantial poem. Having trouble starting? Open with "I remember what it felt like when you held me," and take it from there.

....

....

....

....

....

....

....

....

....

....

....

....

....

....

....

....

....

....

Deep Dive
CHECKING IN OR TUNING OUT?

A word of caution: It is entirely possible to create new destructive patterns that replace the ones we are actively getting rid of. Here, again, vigilance is key. This next exercise is about maintenance. For one week, at the end of each day, select a dominant feeling from the following feeling chart and write that feeling in the subsequent calendar. What I mean by this is, choose whichever feeling came up the most for you on that day and make a note of it. Limit yourself to only one feeling. You may find it interesting to see what feelings are repeaters for you at this stage of the game. Be sure to study the chart before committing to any one feeling for any particular day.

For the most part, today I felt . . .

HAPPY	SAD	ANGRY	OTHER FEELINGS
Calm	Ashamed	Annoyed	Afraid
Cheerful	Awful	Bugged	Anxious
Confident	Disappointed	Destructive	Bored
Content	Discouraged	Disgusted	Confused
Delighted	Gloomy	Frustrated	Curious
Excited	Hurt	Fuming	Embarrassed
Glad	Lonely	Furious	Jealous
Loved	Miserable	Grumpy	Moody
Proud	Sorry	Irritated	Responsible
Relaxed	Unhappy	Mad	Scared
Satisfied	Unloved	Mean	Shy
Silly	Withdrawn	Violent	Uncomfortable
Terrific			Worried
Thankful			
Tickled			

SELF-CARE EVERY DAY

Sometimes self-care takes strategic action. For example, when depressed, it is always a good idea to make your bed in the morning after you wake, if only because you are less apt to climb back into it after you've made it. You can then move on to accomplishing the next productive task of the day.

Our lives have become streamlined with convenience. There's nothing wrong with grabbing something from the freezer, tossing it in the microwave for four minutes, and eating it, but there is also immense satisfaction to be gained from cooking your own meal. Try that one day this week. Wake up, shower, get dressed, and then cook yourself a good breakfast. It doesn't have to happen on a workday. Maybe cook a breakfast meal for yourself on your day off and see how that feels. One of my favorite definitions of adulthood is the ability to delay gratification. Cooking my own meals is a way of seeing this through.

And I must confess, although it didn't in the beginning, today it feels good to do my dishes afterward. Because at some point in time, I decided to grow *all the way up*. I was in a seemingly insurmountable amount of pain when I realized *she* wasn't the one with intimacy issues—I was. And I utterly lacked the self-awareness needed to see that until I'd become so ensconced with Insanity Pain that I had no choice but to look within. And what I discovered within was that I was an adult with very real issues.

None of my healing occurred overnight. I had to surrender day after day to the process, and that began with basic self-care. The reasoning is simple: The love addict spends so much time focusing on their loved one that they lose sight of themselves and their own wants, needs, and desires.

Yes, it's that simple: We are so busy taking care of other people that we stop taking care of ourselves. So while things like self-affirmations seem corny at first, they are a vital part of eliminating the negative self-talk that traps us. The meditations and mindfulness activities may seem like a waste of time, but they allow us precious moments of gainful introspection that allow us to take inventory of our emotional and physical needs and address them compassionately, one by one. Even chores like cleaning and doing laundry contribute to the beautification of our living spaces, making our homes warm, inviting, and pleasing to our eyes while instilling in us a healthy sense of pride and stronger self-esteem.

And then there are the boundaries. We set and defend our boundaries because all of this helps us not get lost in other people, whether the relationship is real or imagined. Boundaries protect us from placing ourselves in a position to be hurt.

I keep saying that vigilance is key. This is because the exercises in this book will get you only so far if you do them once and then cast this workbook aside. I encourage—no, I urge you to sit down and take the time to come up with a daily regimen that incorporates a satisfying routine of daily self-care. Not only because you are worth it but because you deserve to be happy; *you deserve to feel healed and whole within yourself.*

YOUR DEFCON LIST

DEFCON stands for defense readiness condition. Here are some military terms, each a different posture for readiness in regard to national security:

DEFCON 4: Normal, increased intelligence and strengthened security measures. *Alert. Aware. Safe.*

DEFCON 3: Increase in force readiness above normal readiness. *There is a tiny hole in the dam.*

DEFCON 2: Further increase in force readiness but less than maximum readiness. *Worried. Frightened. Things are falling apart.*

DEFCON 1: Maximum force readiness. *All hands on deck. This is NOT a drill.*

Let's apply these vivid images to love addiction. What does the love addict do when we reach DEFCON 2 or 1? What do we do when the crap hits the fan?

Well, for me, I like to have a checklist of things I need to do in order to emotionally reset myself. Not everyone's list is the same, but they all fall under the auspices of basic self-care, especially as it pertains to self-preservation in a tough moment. Creating your list is simple. All you need to do is consider actions that you can do *right now* in order to change your emotional state.

Examples (feel free to add them to your list!):

1. Go to the gym.

2. Do yoga.

3. Watch a favorite movie.

My DEFCON 1 list:

1. ....

2. ....

3. ....

4. ....

5. ....

6. ....

7. ....

8. ....

9. ....

10. ....

This is *your* list: *You* created it. Now you need to remember to use it. You don't have to wait until you are in DEFCON 1 shambles to use it, either; use it whenever you feel emotionally triggered.

This list works best when coupled with your boundaries. If you have promised yourself not to call or text your limerent object, do something on this list instead. If you've decided certain people, places, or things are no longer healthy for you, refer to this list when you feel as if you may violate any boundaries you've set up for yourself in these areas.

You are always allowed to reset yourself at any time you deem necessary. *You are allowed to take your power back.* And these are proven solutions to get you there.

SELF-CARE ACTIVITY TRACKER

I wasn't kidding when I said doing the work was going to take some practice. A tracker is a mindful way for you to develop patterns for self-care that will carry you through the healing process as you move further and further away *from* your addiction and **toward** long-term recovery.

This tracker is important because everything that you're learning (and unlearning) is important. But every love addict needs to have a daily reprieve from the chaos they have unwittingly created in their lives and do something that will get them out of themselves and into the solution.

I've provided a 30-day tracker. In the upper right-hand corner of the tracker, make a note of how many hours of sleep you allowed yourself the night before. Be honest. You'll need to see these numbers in succession to gain an aerial view of how well you actually take care of yourself.

In the body of each calendar day, list the things you did to take care of yourself that day. Go easy on yourself if you can carve out only one or two items. What matters is that you make sure you do something expressly for yourself *every day*.

The goal is to achieve 30 consistent days of basic self-care. If you skip a day, simply start the exercise over. Keep doing it until you can patch together 30 days in a row. You can do it. I know you can. If you're reading this workbook, believe me, you're ready to!

Yoga Cooked for myself	Meditated	Took a walk	Gym Journaled			

OWN YOUR TRUTH

In these past few exercises, we've been focusing on teaching ourselves how to take care of ourselves and recognize that we are human beings who have the right both to ask for what we want out of life and to go out and get it. But action is nothing without awareness. Search your heart and write the responses to the following questions and statements. Remember to divorce yourself from fantasy and take hard looks at what you feel the answers to these questions might be before answering.

I am right here with you, but it falls on you to take this first important step: *Own your truth.*

1. Which of the following symptoms of codependency apply to you?

   ☐ I am not very good at setting boundaries.

   ☐ I am a people pleaser.

   ☐ I feel as if I am responsible for others' emotions.

   ☐ I always ask my partners if things are okay.

   ☐ I am indecisive; I am afraid I will be abandoned if I make the wrong choice.

   ☐ I question or ignore my values in order to connect with my love object.

   ☐ I am usually the one who establishes contact on any given day.

   ☐ I associate being vulnerable and asking for help with weakness.

   ☐ I was taught to never talk about problems outside of the family. It is embarrassing for me to open up with peers when I am suffering.

   ☐ I am someone who judges others, but I have my own serious issues.

2. Now that you are committed to healing through change, what can you do to set healthy boundaries with the people in your life?

....

....

....

....

....

....

....

....

....

3. Think to yourself, "I want to be healthy." What do you need to let go of in order to accomplish this goal?

....

....

....

....

....

....

....

....

....

4. Check the following affirmations that are true for you when you cast aside the beliefs you grew up with and embrace the things you've learned about yourself:

- ☐ I am smart enough to make my own decisions.
- ☐ I can be successful at whatever I do.
- ☐ I am courageous and can stand up for myself.
- ☐ I deserve to be adored.
- ☐ I am funny.
- ☐ I am smart.
- ☐ I am financially responsible.
- ☐ I am patient with myself.
- ☐ I am forgiving of myself.
- ☐ I can trust my inner voice to protect me.
- ☐ I am grateful for the things in my life.
- ☐ I learn from my past.
- ☐ I amaze myself.
- ☐ I am in charge of my life.
- ☐ I am learning to love myself more and more every day.
- ☐ I am worthy of praise.
- ☐ I give good love.
- ☐ I am no longer an underearner and will ask for more money.
- ☐ I believe in myself.
- ☐ I can take care of myself.
- ☐ I am full of positive energy.
- ☐ I am in control of my actions.
- ☐ I am loved.
- ☐ I am lovable.
- ☐ I am a loving person.
- ☐ I am in the process of becoming the best version of myself.
- ☐ I am learning to love my body.
- ☐ I am enough for anyone.
- ☐ I am safe.
- ☐ I am proud of who I am.
- ☐ I am creative.
- ☐ I am wanted.
- ☐ I am a good friend to myself.
- ☐ I am gentle with myself.
- ☐ I am important.

KEY TAKEAWAYS AND REFLECTIONS

It has become evident in my practice that being human and embracing our humanity are the secret goals of every love addict. The love addict is a complication of seemingly desperate need that masks itself as desire. We need for *them* to love us, but that love comes with conditions because, more often than not, when the limerent object conforms to our wishes, we suddenly find ourselves not wanting them anymore, and our eye wanders.

I have found that the solution is for the love addict to evolve and develop into someone who is self-sufficient—someone who doesn't *need* anyone to like them because they have found a way to like or love themselves. This newfound independence can be accomplished only when the love addict embraces a willingness to be brave: to be vulnerable within the confines of their very human condition and investigate new avenues toward becoming their authentic selves.

The love addict can say they love themselves, but without backing that statement up with actions, it's just lip service. We heal through action that is born from compassionate awareness, and that awareness is experienced when you set boundaries, protect yourself, and forgive yourself, and understand that loving yourself also means facing the things you hate most about yourself so you can abolish those things and live the life you're meant to live.

Everything you came here looking *for*, you came here looking *with*.

CHAPTER SEVEN

Keep Up the Momentum

Y ou have embarked on a brave new journey as you conquer your love addiction and reclaim your power, and there are count-less different ways to take the knowledge that's out there (and in this book) and bend it to your will, transforming it into new and creative ways to practice self-care and self-love on a daily basis. All you need to do is continue to do the work and use your limitless imagination.

TODAY AND BEYOND

Radio talk show personality Gary Chapman teaches that there are five primary love languages. His argument is that people tend to express love in these five fundamental ways:

1. Words of affirmation

2. Quality time

3. Gifts

4. Acts of service

5. Physical touch

Words of affirmation

When words of affirmation are spoken with authenticity or compassion, they resound within one's soul for years and years. To this day, I still remember almost every positive word that's ever been spoken to me. I love it when family and friends support me and encourage me to do difficult and challenging things. But it wasn't until I identified as a love addict that I realized I never spoke any words of encouragement to myself with any authenticity. Left to my own devices, I would have given up on myself a long time ago. But I found people who told me not only that it was possible for me to overcome my dyslexia and succeed but also that I didn't have the right to not even try. Later in life, those voices replaced the ones I'd grown up with, and I learned to let them love me until I could love myself. And once I did, there was a huge space created in my life that would happily accommodate the woman who would someday become my wife.

Quality time

Quality time is a language that revolves around togetherness, but I think it's also about being complete within yourself. It's the mindfulness we've talked about; it's also about carving out time for yourself so you can check in with yourself emotionally and really be in touch with where you're at. It's about unplugging, or turning off and tuning in, as we used to say in the '60s: It's about "me" time.

Gifts

The notion of gifts as a love language is a tricky one unless you look at it from a financial perspective. You and I live in a world of commerce where everyone has to eke out a living and pay bills. But basic self-care and self-love suggest otherwise. When you get paid, before you pay your bills, make sure you set aside some money to pay *yourself*. You don't need to break the bank to do it. It could mean setting aside a couple of dollars to take a bus ride to a park or a zoo, or maybe go see that movie you've been excited about.

Acts of service

Chapman's ideas regarding acts of service encompass all the things you could do for your loved one in an attempt to bring the two of you closer together. But what if you did a few things for *yourself* that yielded the same results? Cooking a nice meal for yourself would fall into this category, or cleaning your car, or even treating yourself to that long-overdue trip to the doctor's office. These all fall under the umbrella of self-love and self-care; they also contribute to feelings of pride about who you are and what you can accomplish when you aren't making it all about *them*.

Physical touch

The love language of physical touch requires intimacy, but I'd dare say intimacy is merely a means to an end. Hugging and cuddling are both physical actions that trigger the release of the love hormone oxytocin into our bodies. Despite it being the purview of infants everywhere, oxytocin can also be produced by socializing with family and friends. We hug our loved ones when we greet them, and this releases oxytocin into our system, but there are now over-the-counter remedies for those instances where you need to be physically comforted yet cannot engage with other people. Weighted blankets simulate pressure from being hugged or swaddled. Wrap yourself up in one of these while watching television or reading a good book (or journaling) and you will discover how good it feels to hug yourself!

Deep Dive
MAKING UP YOUR MIND

For this exercise, we will examine and work on your ability to make decisions. Love addicts usually fall prey to a codependent aspect of people-pleasing that renders them afraid to make their own decisions (for fear of having that be the reason for a fictional negative consequence).

In order for this to work, once every few days, you will need to look inward and identify the moments in your life when you relied on someone else to make a decision. Examine each situation and write about them here. I've listed a couple of examples to start you off.

INSTANCE	REASONING
I couldn't choose a restaurant, so we ate at that place I hate so much.	I am always afraid he won't like me. If he doesn't like me, he may leave me for someone else.
I didn't help plan Becky's birthday party.	I was worried she wouldn't like it and they would blame me.

Deep Dive

THE I'S HAVE IT

This exercise is challenging because it's all about getting out of your comfort zone–but that's what you've been doing, right? Establishing your independence is important, especially for someone who has traditionally been very worried about what other people think and feel. For this exercise, I want you to find three things to do on your own that you would normally want someone else to do with you. Maybe it means trying a new pottery class at the community center or eating at a really nice restaurant alone. Or maybe it's simply going to a movie alone. Any of these things are fine, but I'd really like you to use your imagination and come up with three things that speak to you, *and then go do them*.

   Afterward, reflect. How did you feel when you started out with this activity? How did you feel after you'd checked each item off the list? Write your experience down.

ACTIVITY: _____

EXPERIENCE: ....

....

....

....

....

....

....

....

....

....

....

ACTIVITY: _____

EXPERIENCE: ....

....

....

....

....

....

....

....

....

....

ACTIVITY: _____

EXPERIENCE: ....

....

....

....

....

....

....

....

....

....

WHAT TO DO IF YOU'RE STILL STRUGGLING

None of this is easy. But this is not to say that there is a grading curve on recovery. People come in all shapes and sizes, and some readers may discover that despite the work, they are still suffering. Your first call to action that I encourage is to find a good therapist. And by *good*, I don't necessarily mean one with a Harvard education. I mean someone you feel you can trust with your stuff—someone you believe will help you examine all of it in an intelligent and insightful way. If you have a meeting with a therapist and things don't click, trust your feelings, thank them for their time, and continue your search. Do not people-please yourself into years of costly therapy that won't help you tackle this vital issue. Not now, when you are finally ready to recover.

The work is to stay on top of your triggers so you can continue to set boundaries and address that needy part of you that starts to feel abandoned by someone you've met. It is my experience that you will always be attracted to the unavailable, but the difference will be that you won't chase them anymore and you will have become more aware of that needy energy that comes up in you and know how to channel it.

Ultimately, you will regain your power by not losing yourself in love addiction. Part of this is in acknowledging that nothing has to happen right away. For the alcoholic, sobriety is the key to successful living. For the love addict, *slow*briety is where it's at. Try not to rush into anything. Take your time and invest in your wellness practices to get to know how you really feel about a person before impulsively opening up the floodgates. *Don't paint your red flags green.*

Bear in mind that I am taking into account the power of our more basic instincts. Desire, lust, seduction, and fantasy all fuel the love addict's frenzied need for the "love fix." True connection is about having a healthy sense of self that manifests in a way that guarantees that there is nothing anyone has to offer—not sex, not money, not attention, nor approval—that can make you compromise your commitment to being your genuine, authentic self at all times. After all, it is this authentic self that your prospective partner should meet and fall in love with.

And that always takes time.

PHILLIP'S DILEMMA,
PART 2

My work with Phillip spanned almost eight months, with the two of us meeting twice a week as he danced between love addiction and sex addiction. Phillip's goals were clear-cut: He wanted a long-term relationship but was helplessly avoidant, drawing upon the same emotional cues as a child with a magnifying glass intent on destroying every ant he encountered. In looking back over his life, we were able to determine why he was locked into the same self-destructive pattern of behavior, but helping him amend that behavior was met with a lot of backsliding as he repeatedly sabotaged seemingly fruitful unions. The breaking point, however, was an argument he had with a woman he was dating. The two were locking horns over her mistrust of his spending time with a sexy coworker, a dynamic he'd introduced into the relationship as a reason for ending things. Thankfully, Phillip was able to see his part in it, and so we were able to devise a way for Phillip to communicate how much he valued her companionship and the work he was doing to create a lasting relationship with this woman. She was, after all, responding to ideas he himself had so cavalierly placed in her head, so her fears of his infidelity, although unrealistic—Phillip had no intention of ever cheating on her—were not unfounded. Phillip was able to apologize for his insensitivity, and the two of them agreed to start fresh, with him understanding that his job was to remain loving as they explored their connection; hers was to release her grip on his sex life and trust him to not abandon her. As of this writing, the two have been together for almost three months (a record for Phillip).

Deep Dive
MY PRECIOUS

The love addict tends to hoard items of sentimental value in order to per-petuate the fantasy that a relationship that was inherently bad for them was actually romantic and worth clinging to. Photographs, social media sites, mementos, and souvenirs plague the love addict. For the battered house-wife, the cherishing of photos taken during happier times reinforce neural pathways and compel her to continue to text and associate with someone who is cruel to her. The cheated-on man will retain and cherish opera ticket stubs or a gifted wristwatch that he will pore over to ruminate on how deep their love was, despite the ease with which she left him for another man.

Our work here on grief and loss has prepared many of you to begin the process of letting go. For some, this will seem a more arduous task than it will be for others, but again, baby steps are important.

First, make a list of what you need to let go of (old scrapbooks, photos in your cell phone or laptop, favorite restaurants or bars the two of you used to frequent, etc.). This is a big move, so take your time with it. I am not saying you need to get rid of everything, and if it's too painful to do, you don't need to get rid of anything at all; old photos can easily be placed in a shoebox under your bed, and pictures on your phone can be moved to a USB drive. But you need to establish your independence and mark your boundary as a separate entity that exists *outside of the relationship*. Find a new favorite restaurant or bar in order to pave new neural pathways. Reflect for a short while and then, when you are ready, make a list of five things you are ready to let go of.

1. ....

....

2. ....

....

3. ....

....

4. ....

....

5. ....

....

Now that your list is complete, choose one thing to follow through on, and get rid of it right now. If you've the strength to conquer the whole list, my hat is off to you. But, like I said, this last part is about baby steps—you need to select only one.

Write a letter to the item(s) or place(s) here, explaining why this separation needs to happen. Be as honest as possible. If you throw away the item(s), throw away the letter. If you keep the item, keep the letter with it.

We are not striving for closure here; *we are striving for completion*. Every relationship has a beginning, a middle, and an end. And so does your suffering.

....

....

....

....

....

....

....

....

....

....

....

....

....

....

....

....

....

....

....

....

....

....

....

....

Deep Dive
ROUND, ROUND, GET AROUND, I GET AROUND

What happens when the love addict is no longer feeding their addiction? In some cases, the love addict may develop what is called a *process addiction*: a new way of processing feelings with the potential for equally disastrous results. For this reason, at this crucial stage in their recovery, the love addict will become like a mouse in a maze. Looking for anything else that will distract them from this restless need to reattach to their love object, they will cling wholly to other outside influences. Sex, food, shopping, cigarettes, alcohol, drugs, video games, crossword puzzles . . . the love addict will consume these and more with a vengeance if they are not invested in the work.

To stop any process addictions from gaining a foothold, it is vital that the love addict find someone to trust. This last exercise is the formation of a contract you will make with yourself. You will need a witness, and that's where the person you trust comes in. If things get out of hand, or if you appear to be suffering, this person will advise you to seek professional help, and they will use this final document as a testament to the agreement. Remember to be as honest as possible to be thorough.

In my idea of a healthy relationship, I need:

1. ....

2. ....

3. ....

4. ....

5. ....

6. ....

7. ....

These are my recognized signs of an unhealthy relationship
(my boundaries):

1. ....

2. ....

3. ....

4. ....

5. ....

6. ....

7. ....

KEY TAKEAWAYS AND REFLECTIONS

I truly wish there was something I could impart to you that would make closing this workbook easier. I need you to know that these exercises aren't merely exercises; many of them are lifestyle choices you will need to adopt in order to have and enjoy healthy relationships.

I also want you to know there are other resources out there that you can avail yourself of. If you own a smartphone, there are self-care and self-love activity tracker apps that will help you stay true to the work by correcting your course when things begin to go sideways. See the Resources section (page 169) for some suggestions. But I also want to let you know that you don't need them to transform your life.

Everything you need to be happy is inside you already.

I promise you, you've only scratched the surface. More will be revealed. Be brave and be vulnerable, and investigate what drives you. More importantly, believe the answers your heart tells you. You have always been courageous and smart and strong and wonderful. But somewhere along the way, you learned to tell yourself that you aren't and started believing that only someone else could determine your value. Never, ever fall for that lie again. And don't ever rely on someone else's feelings to determine your own.

Your feelings are just fine. All you have to do is feel them, identify them . . . *And trust them.*

Dr. Howard Samuels
March 2021

Resources

——

GRATEFUL: This app works as a gratitude journal in your pocket. Prompts will allow you to record what you're grateful for each day and, over time, will rewire your brain to focus on the positive and feel more optimistic.

I AM: This fully customizable affirmations app allows you to set how many times during the day you want to see an affirmation. The affirmations will pop up on your phone screen throughout your day in appropriate and wonderful ways.

MEND: Mend offers self-care support to help you get through tough breakups. If you are heartbroken, their personalized program will help you feel better faster.

MOODPATH: If you struggle with negative thoughts or feelings, this mental health app will gently guide you through exercises to improve your emotional well-being.

SHINE: This app, specifically tailored for women, sends motivational messages to your phone based on your personalized self-care goals, inspiring confidence under pressure.

TALKSPACE: This online therapy app lets you have video or voice sessions with licensed therapists for a much lower cost than traditional in-person therapy. As of this writing, plans start at $49 per week.

References

Chapman, Gary. *The 5 Love Languages*. Chicago: Northfield Publishing, 2010.

James, John and Russell Friedman. *The Grief Recovery Handbook*. New York: William Morrow, 2017.

Katehakis, Alexandra. "Sex and Love Addiction: What's the Difference?" *Psychology Today*. Last modified June 28, 2011. PsychologyToday.com/us /blog/sex-lies-trauma/201106/sex-and-love-addiction-whats-the-difference.

Schneiderman, Inna, Orna Zagoory-Sharon, James F. Leckman, and Ruth Feldman. "Oxytocin during the Initial Stages of Romantic Attachment: Relations to Couples' Interactive Reciprocity." *Psychoneuroendocrinology* 37, 8 (August 2012): 1277–85. DOI.org/10.1016/j.psyneuen.2011.12.021.

Tennov, Dorothy. *Love and Limerence*, 2nd ed. Lanham, MD: Scarborough House, 1998.

Index

A

Acceptance, 21
Accountabili-buddies, 21, 36
Action steps, 35, 38
Acts of service love
    language, 157
Addiction, 1–2. *See also*
    Love addiction
Affirmations, 20, 52,
    61, 64–66, 153
Angelou, Maya, 12, 23
Anxious attachment, 34
Attachment theory,
    34–35, 37
Avoidant attachment, 35

B

Beck, Aaron, 44
Behavioral patterns, 127
Being right, 50
Beliefs
  changing, 60–61
  core, 62–63
  and distorted
    thinking, 43–51
Blaming, 49
Boundary-setting, 114–119
Bowlby, John, 34

C

Catastrophizing, 45, 47
Chapman, Gary, 156
Codependency,
    102–104, 151

Cognitive
    distortions, 44–51
Cognitive
    reappraisal, 81–82
Color Purple, The (film), 71
Communication, 120–123
Compatibility, 105–107
Control fallacies, 48
Courage, 23

D

"Dear John" letter, 91–92
Decision-making, 158
Defense readiness
    condition
    (DEFCON), 147–148
Distorted thinking, 43–51
Dopamine, 10, 18

E

Emotional
    intelligence, 41, 71
Emotional
    reasoning, 44, 49
Emotions
  emotional Rolodex
    exercise, 93–94
  labeling, 71–75
  managing, 89–90, 95–96
  noticing repeating, 144
  regulating, 79–80
  triggers, 1, 76–77
  understanding, 69–70, 97

F

Fallacy of change, 50
Fallacy of fairness, 48
Feeling Wheel, 72–73
Feelings. *See* Emotions
Filtering, 46
Forgiveness, 57–58, 60–61

G

Gifts love language, 157
Global labeling, 50
Goal-setting, 31–33, 35
Gratitude, 139–140
Grief, 85–88

H

Heaven's reward fallacy, 51
Honesty, 120

I

Independence, 159–160

J

Johnson, Sharon L., 46
Jung, Carl, 137

K

Katehakis, Alexandra, 4

L

Labeling, 45
Letting go, 163–165
Lieberman, Matthew D., 71

Liespotting (Meyer), 70
Limerence, 99–100
Loss, 85–88
Love addiction
  cycle, 9–10, 15–17
  defined, 1–3
  recovery from, 21–22, 25–26, 34–38
  self-quiz, 5–8
  vs. sex addiction, 4
Love and Limerence (Tennov), 99
Love languages, 156–157
Lying, to yourself, 70

M

Meditation, 83–84
Memories, 27–30, 141–143
Meyer, Pamela, 70
Mind reading, 47
Mindfulness, 129–131
Mistakes, 121

N

Needs, 129
Neural pathways, 18

O

Overgeneralization, 45, 47
Oxytocin, 10, 157

P

Personalization, 44, 48
Physical touch love language, 157
Polarized thinking, 44, 46
Process addiction, 166

Q

Quality time love language, 156

R

Recovery, 21–22, 25–26, 34–38
Relationships
  codependent, 102–104
  compatibility in, 105–107

healthy vs. unhealthy, 166–167
  ideal, 111–112
  ideas about, 52
  love addiction effect on, 99–101
  memories of past, 28–30
  two-week tracking exercise, 12–14
Repetition, 18

S

Secure attachment, 34
Self-care
  activity tracker, 149–150
  check-ins, 132–133
  daily, 145–146
  importance of, 129
  obstacles to, 134–135
Self-compassion, 137–138, 154
Self-talk, 137–138
Sex addiction, 4
Shame, 26
Shoulds, 49
Support systems, 21, 36

T

Tennov, Dorothy, 99
Therapist's Guide to Clinical Intervention (Johnson), 46
Therapy, 161
Thoughts
  cognitive distortions, 44–51
  negative, 53–55
  positive, 56
Triggers, 1, 31, 76–77, 161
Truth, owning your, 151–153

V

Validation, 108–110
Values, 124–126

W

Willcox, Gloria, 72
Words of affirmation love language, 156
Wyrick, Dominee, 76

About the Author

**Dr. Howard C. Samuels** is a licensed therapist with a doctorate in clinical psychology who has worked in the field of addiction for over 30 years. He has run and operated three world-renowned treatment centers while maintaining a successful private practice in the Los Angeles area. Dr. Samuels specializes in the treatment of mood and addictive disorders, love addiction, and substance abuse intervention. One of the most sought-after addiction professionals in the nation, Dr. Samuels has appeared on ABC's *Good Morning America*, NBC's *Today*, CBS, CNN, *Larry King Live*, and *Entertainment Tonight* as well as syndicated radio programs to speak about his professional and personal experience with recovery.